THROUGH THE WINDOW

The Great Western Railway
from
Paddington to Penzance
1924

300 miles of English countryside
as seen from GWR trains on the
Cornish Riviera Route

OLD HOUSE BOOKS
Moretonhampstead Devon

Old House Books produce facsimile copies of long out of print maps and books that we believe deserve a second innings. Our reprints of Victorian and Edwardian maps and guide books are of interest to genealogists and local historians. Other titles have been chosen to explore the character of life in years gone by and are helpful to anyone who wishes to know a bit more about the lives of their ancestors, whether they were respectable gentlewomen, early tourists, commuters on the first railways or even perhaps cunning poachers.

For details of other Old House Books titles please visit our website www.OldHouseBooks.co.uk or request a catalogue.

Through The Window was first published by The Great Western Railway Company in 1924 and reprinted up until the Second World War.

Jacket illustration by Stuart Humphrey based on the
GWR poster '100 Years of Progress 1835–1935'
by Murray Secretan
showing King Charles II with the Cornish Riviera Express
passing the Parson and Clerk rock between
Dawlish and Teignmouth in Devon. *See page 80.*

This edition, including twenty GWR pages from
Bradshaw's timetable, was published in 2008 by
© Old House Books
The Old Police Station, Pound Street, Moretonhampstead,
Devon TQ13 8PA UK
Tel: 01647 440707   Fax: 01647 440202
info@OldHouseBooks.co.uk   www.OldHouseBooks.co.uk
ISBN 978 1 873590 75 1

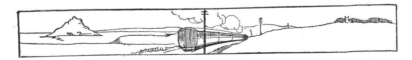

HOW TO USE "THROUGH THE WINDOW"

THE journey of 305 miles from Paddington to Penzance is much more than a means to an end. It is an experience thoroughly worth while for its own sake. It unfolds a vast stretch of English landscape in constantly changing panorama and traverses almost the entire breadth of England at its widest part.

In this book an attempt has been made to break up this long journey into its component parts in the geographical sense. Any such system of grouping is open to objections, but there seem to be good logical grounds for the following rough classification :

Within these main divisions, points and features of interest seen through the carriage windows are described in such detail as space will allow. Some tell their own story, others become interesting when one reads of origins and associations not obvious on the surface.

Each page of the detailed letterpress covers as nearly as possible six miles of the line and is faced by a map of the same section on which points of interest are identified by reference numbers corresponding to those used in the text. The terms left and right used throughout the book mean the left and right of a passenger who is sitting facing the engine.

The maps are to be read from the bottom upwards, as this makes their direction coincide with that of the train as the book is held by a passenger looking towards Penzance. The letterpress, however, is read in the ordinary way.

The fact that the famous " 10-30 Limited," the Cornish Riviera Express by which those who make the full journey from London to Penzance usually travel, makes a non-stop run from Paddington to Plymouth, a distance of 225 miles, is sufficient in itself to excite interest in the mechanical side of such a splendid achievement—in the powerful express locomotive and the finely appointed corridor coaches behind it, in the splendid track which makes the journey pass so smoothly and with so little consciousness of terrific speed, in the pick-up water troughs and other pieces of equipment which represent the last word up to date in railway engineering.

In this book there is no room for any substantial measure of information about those things, but they are described in detail and admirably illustrated in another publication of the Great Western Railway, " The 10-30 Limited—a book for boys of all ages."

LONDON.

THE
OUTSKIRTS
OF
LONDON

Paddington Station.   E Margaret Holman.

THE GATEWAY TO THE WEST

PADDINGTON Station is London's great gateway to the West, and the fascination of travel begins from the momen one arrives beneath the vast curves of its great glass roof. The people on the platforms, the scraps of conversation, the destination boards on the trains, the labels on the luggage—all have a strong West Country flavour. A dash of naval uniform conjures up visions of distant Plymouth and Devonport. The characteristic *patois* of Devon and Somerset mingles with the dialect of West Cornwall, which has at times a quaint, musical note and brings into play local words that only a Cornishman would understand.

This long, swift journey from London to Land's End—or as near to it as makes no matter—has about it a certain savour of romance, a spice of adventure, which no amount of familiarity with railway travelling can destroy. Not only the great distance in itself—over 300 miles—but also the fact that so vast a stretch of it is taken at a single stride helps to create the feeling that in stepping on to the footboard of the " 10-30 Limited " one is embarking upon an adventure, and that's a fine thing in itself.

No need to enquire which platform for the Cornish Riviera Express—Number One every time ! To experienced travellers, Paddington Station stands out among the London termini by a certain coherence of arrangement, and Platform Number One is in many ways a model of convenience, grouping together all the facilities one needs at the outset of a long journey.

One steps aboard the " Limited " with a sensation not far removed from that of boarding a sea-going ship. There is a certain irrevocability about it which makes the undertaking a vastly different one from a journey on the Underground, where you can change your mind and retrieve your position within a few minutes of starting. To put it in another way, this great journey to the West has something of the fascination of foreign travel. Land's End has a far-away sound when one is surrounded by the surging crowds and noisy bustle of London, but no farther away than London seems when one is walking the Promenade at Penzance.

And now steam is up, and a vast pile of luggage has been stowed away in the holds of the good ship " Limited," the last hand-shakes are taken and the last " Good-byes " said as the guard blows his whistle and waves his green flag, and dead on the stroke of 10-30 a.m. the long train begins to move and will not cease from moving until we draw into Plymouth North Road Station, 225 miles away, at 2.37 p.m. precisely. We shall, however, shake off several parts of our tail *en route*—"slip" coaches for Weymouth, Taunton, Ilfracombe, Minehead, Exeter and other intermediate places.

PADDINGTON TO EALING BROADWAY

THE first half dozen miles of the journey from PADDINGTON (1) lie through the western suburbs of London. Now London has some very pleasant western suburbs, but it is too much to expect to see them at their best from the train, for London has a habit—a very unwise one, considering the kind of first impression it gives to strangers arriving in the capital—of showing her worst side to the railway. But Suburbia, with her tall houses blocking out wider views, forms only an infinitesimal stage of our more than 300 miles run to the West, and by the time one has got comfortably settled in one's seat the solid rampart of houses on either side of the line has been left behind.

ROYAL OAK STATION (2) and the important suburban station of WESTBOURNE PARK (3) are passed within the first two or three minutes and then some points of interest begin to appear on either side. On the right is a peep at KENSAL GREEN CEMETERY (4), where Thackeray, Leigh Hunt and other famous people are buried. Only one or two of the stones show from the railway, and the glimpse of trees rising above walls and fences is suggestive of a park rather than a cemetery.

Wormwood Scrubbs

The large open space seen on the left, with a great airship shed upon it, is WORMWOOD SCRUBBS (5), and the large range of buildings behind in the barrack style of architecture are those of the big convict prison of Wormwood Scrubbs. The prison was built by convict labour and has room for about fourteen hundred prisoners. During the War, however, Wormwood Scrubbs was an important station of the Royal Air Force.

Behind Wormwood Scrubbs may be seen rather farther away some of the tall cupolas of the great Shepherd's Bush EXHIBITION BUILDINGS (6) which were used for the Japan-British, the Franco-British and other exhibitions a few years before the War, but which have become more or less derelict since. At a distance of 4½ miles from Paddington we pass through the populous suburb of ACTON (7), which gives us a momentary vision of open country looking across to the right towards the spire of HARROW-ON-THE-

Towards Harrow

HILL (8). But the view is soon shut off by the widespread brick-and-mortar of EALING (9), one of the largest and most important of the western suburbs.

EALING BROADWAY (10) is as far as the "Tube" trains venture out of London in this direction, and one or more of them is usually seen in the station to the right.

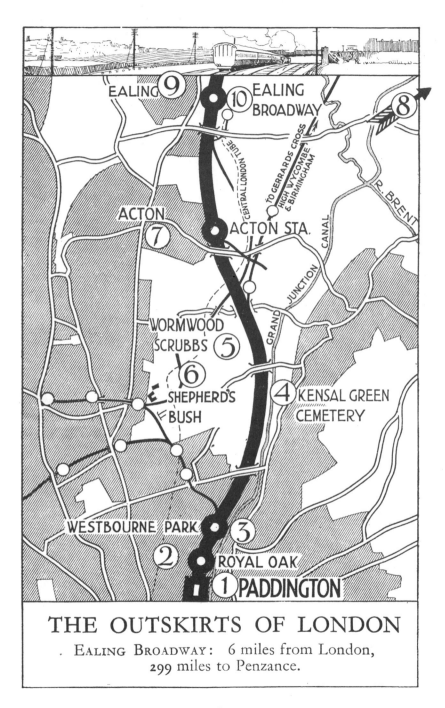

THE OUTSKIRTS OF LONDON

. EALING BROADWAY: 6 miles from London,
299 miles to Penzance.

EALING TO WEST DRAYTON

Hanwell Asylum

FEW things impress the traveller more when leaving the metropolis by this route than the extraordinary extent to which "wireless" has captured suburban London. Practically every back garden has its aerial.

Beyond WEST EALING STATION (1), Hanwell Recreation Ground on the right opens out a wider prospect in that direction, and beyond HANWELL AND ELTHORNE STATION (2) the tower of HANWELL CHURCH (3) shows up on the same side of the line and is of interest because in its churchyard lies Jonas Hanway, the man who, braving contemporary ridicule, introduced the umbrella into this country about 1750.

The line now crosses the RIVER BRENT (4), a winding tributary of the Thames, which it enters at BRENTFORD (5), the old county town of Middlesex, a couple of miles across country to the left. It must be confessed that the most imposing feature of Hanwell is the great LUNATIC ASYLUM (6) of the County of London set above the west bank of the Brent to the left of the railway. We are travelling now over a long viaduct which strides across the Brent Valley and in a few moments cross the OXFORD ROAD (7), which we have already noticed alongside on the left, with its tram route and heavy stream of traffic. This road is the direct continuation of the fashionable shopping centre of Oxford Street. It goes west *via* Uxbridge to Oxford and over the Cotswold Hills into Gloucestershire.

The Oxford Road

Looking across country to the right we have a splendid view of HARROW-ON-THE-HILL (8) rising out of the landscape like an Italian hill city, crowned by the spire of its ancient church. In the middle distance is seen a cluster of tall wireless masts. At SOUTHALL (9) the great Maypole margarine factory adjoins the railway on the left, and other names famous in commerce mark modern factories set close beside the line in the next few miles.

Just beyond Southall we cross the GRAND JUNCTION CANAL (10) with bridges, barges and ducks all doing their best to make it picturesque. At HAYES and HARLINGTON STATION (11) the enormous buildings in which " His Master's Voice" gramophones are made stand close to the railway.

Factories at Hayes

The country has now assumed a pleasantly open character, with old farmsteads and quaint cottages showing up at intervals, while fine rows of elms are characteristic of the Hayes district.

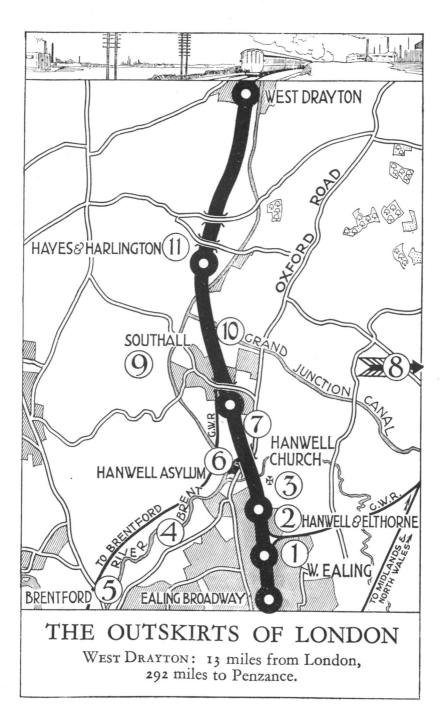

THE OUTSKIRTS OF LONDON

WEST DRAYTON: 13 miles from London,
292 miles to Penzance.

11

WEST DRAYTON TO SLOUGH

Cowley & Colne River

AT West Drayton and Yiewsley Station (1) the former village lies to the left and the latter to the right of the railway. From this station a branch line turns off to the right for the pleasant flourishing old town of Uxbridge (2) which is about two miles north from here. Almost immediately the River Colne (3), which marks the frontier between Middlesex and Buckinghamshire, is crossed, and a second channel of the same stream passes under the railway soon afterwards, the two meeting at West Drayton.

The church spire now seen on the right is that of Cowley (4) mid-way to Uxbridge, and the old tower of Iver Church (5) shows up a little farther along on the same side. We are now in " beautiful Bucks " and although the country is still inclined to be flat it is well timbered, especially in the distance to the left, where part of the broad expanse of Windsor Great Forest (6) is seen covering the higher ground which forms the horizon in that direction.

The Grand Junction Canal (7) is again seen drawing close up to the railway on the right just before we pass through Langley Station (8). Beyond it are the oak woods of Langley Park (9), the residence of Sir R. Harvey, while on the left appears the old church tower of Langley Marish (10).

Langley Marish Church

We are well clear of London now and factories have given place to agriculture. Such a village as Langley is definitely rural, and grazing cattle give the landscape a touch of active life.

Across country to the left, slightly less than a couple of miles from the railway, the grey pile of Windsor Castle (11) rises out of the Thames Valley, its long array of towers and battlements drawn out in full broadside from this view-point. The Castle, or at least part of it, has been a royal residence since the Norman Conquest. The great Round Tower forms the largest unit in this imposing group of buildings.

Windsor Castle

The River Thames (12) divides Windsor from its close and no less famous neighbour Eton (13), but the buildings of the historic public school cannot be picked out with any certainty from the railway. Slough (14) is an old country town which has been modernised a good deal in recent years. This is the junction for Windsor, the branch line turning off to the left.

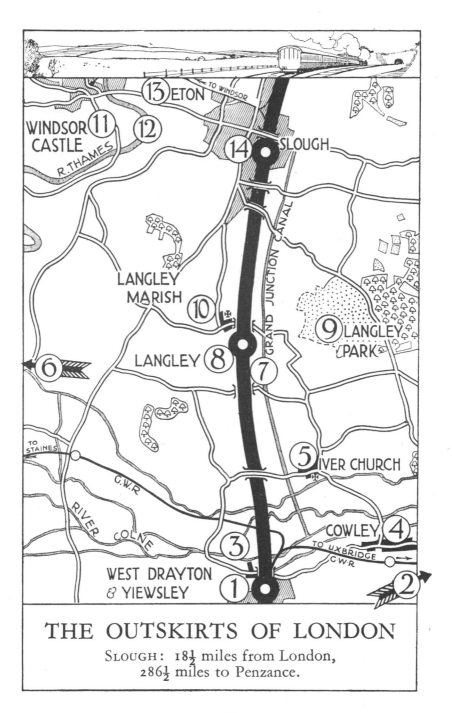

THE OUTSKIRTS OF LONDON

SLOUGH: 18½ miles from London,
286½ miles to Penzance.

WINDSOR CASTLE.

THE
THAMES
VALLEY

The Thames.   E. Margaret Holman.

THE THAMES VALLEY

ONE of the fascinations of this journey to the West is to mark how the English countryside divides itself into a variety of types, some typical in a broad sense of England as a whole, others sharply defined and characteristic only of themselves. Cornwall for instance, is so different from the rest of England as to be a distinct country rather than a county. Parts of Somerset are more typical of Holland than of England.

But here in the Thames Valley the fascination of the countryside lies in the fact that it is the most English part of England. It is a country in miniature, holding within itself all that is most characteristic of England and the English. How could it be otherwise when the Thames Valley holds Windsor, the home of English kings and queens of many dynasties; Runnymede, the birthplace of English liberties; Oxford and Eton, the cradles of our public education and the generating stations of English character, and Henley standing for the sporting instinct in us? Every historic phase of English life and most modern ones, too, can be illustrated by typical instances from the valley of the Thames.

No wonder, then, that the quiet pastoral landscape through which we shall travel for twenty miles or so should have inspired the one piece of literature which interprets more perfectly, perhaps, than any other, the essential and abiding spirit of rural England. Gray's "Elegy in a Country Churchyard" was written at Stoke Poges, only three or four miles across country to the north of Slough. There, bosomed in trees, is the veritable churchyard of the "Elegy" and the tomb of Thomas Gray. The spire of Stoke Poges church is only seen as a distant and fleeting glimpse from the railway, but we shall pass close beside other old country churches where Gray might just as easily have found the scene which answered to his mood. In any case, it is impossible to travel through the Thames Valley by this route, crossing and re-crossing the river and running through the lush meadowland which borders it on either side, without seeing from time to time

"the lowing herd wind slowly o'er the lea."

London itself is in the Thames Valley in the broader sense, but this stage of our journey commences in a more realistic way at Slough, where Windsor Castle marks the river only two miles away and because from here to Reading we are in intimate touch with this broad stream of English history that winds itself slowly through the most typical of all English landscapes, with grand woodlands banking up from the water at frequent intervals and the whole countryside dotted with pleasant homesteads and picturesque old villages.

SLOUGH TO MAIDENHEAD

Stoke Poges Church.

WITH a sharp eye it is possible to catch a glimpse of the stumpy spire of STOKE POGES CHURCH (1) rising above the trees about two miles across country to the right immediately after leaving Slough. The churchyard of Stoke Poges has been given a world-wide fame in Gray's "Elegy in a Country Churchyard," which was written in this peaceful spot where the poet himself lies close to the east end of the church.

On both sides of the line are seen parts of what is now the SLOUGH TRADING ESTATE (2), occupying the site of the motor transport "dump" which was established during the latter part of the War for the repair and re-conditioning of the thousands of motor lorries incapacitated on active service, and which, after the Armistice, was the subject of much comment on account of the vast sums of public money sunk in this alleged "white elephant."

Windsor Castle is still the most prominent landmark to the left as we travel forward through the Thames Valley, with the RIVER (3) gradually bending its course towards us—if one may reverse the logical order of things for the sake of descriptive convenience. BURNHAM BEECHES STATION (4), which is just 21 miles from London, suggests by its name the near presence of the glorious tract of woodland which has been since 1879, and will be for evermore, the cherished possession of the citizens of London,

Taplow Church

who flock out here by thousands at holiday times. BURNHAM BEECHES (5) form the principal expanse of woodland within easy reach of the metropolis.

BURNHAM VILLAGE (6) is marked by the church spire now seen on the right. The great BATH ROAD (7), from London to Bath, has been fairly close alongside on the left all the way from Slough, and passes under the railway just beyond TAPLOW STATION (8). The spire of TAPLOW CHURCH (9) is seen on the right, with the splendid mansion of TAPLOW COURT (10), Lord Desborough's seat, showing up prominently on the hill farther north.

A mile across country to the left is seen the tower of BRAY CHURCH (11), once in the charge of the immortal Vicar of Bray,

Towards Bray

who, if the popular ballad is trustworthy, changed his opinions as often and as easily as he changed his coat.

Now we cross the Thames for the first time and enter Berkshire. The main arches of the bridge which carries the railway across the river are said to be the widest brick-spans in the world.

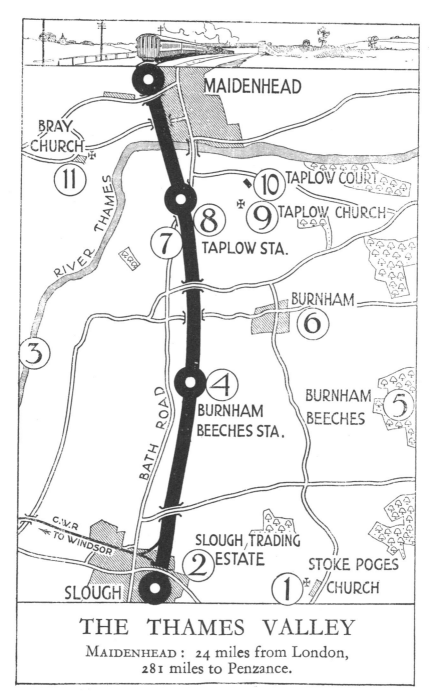

THE THAMES VALLEY

MAIDENHEAD : 24 miles from London,
281 miles to Penzance.

Map labels: MAIDENHEAD, BRAY CHURCH, TAPLOW COURT, TAPLOW CHURCH, TAPLOW STA., RIVER THAMES, BURNHAM, BURNHAM BEECHES, BURNHAM BEECHES STA., BATH ROAD, G.W.R. TO WINDSOR, SLOUGH, SLOUGH TRADING ESTATE, STOKE POGES CHURCH

MAIDENHEAD TO TWYFORD

Shottesbrooke Steeple

LOOKING up-river—that is, to the right—as we cross the Thames, the fine lines of MAIDENHEAD BRIDGE (1) can be admired at close range. This handsome stone structure carries the main road from London to Bath across the river from Buckinghamshire into Berkshire. A short distance beyond it is the famous BOULTER'S LOCK (2), one of the chief focus-points of the gay life of the river at any fine week-end in summer, when the lock is crowded with punts, rowing boats and motor launches, all made gorgeous by the presence in great numbers and infinite variety of one of the most fascinating of English types—the up-river girl.

The fine bank of trees seen on the right beyond the bridge is part of CLIVEDEN WOODS (3) ,which figure on the map as a sort of western extension of Burnham Beeches running right down to the water's edge. The high ground in the distance beyond the woods marks the southern edge of the CHILTERN HILLS (4) in the Beaconsfield neighbourhood.

By the time we have noted all these things we are running through the long drawn-out town of MAIDENHEAD (5), which begins immediately the river is crossed. At first it simply provides a narrow border on either side of the Bath Road, but grows broader towards its western end, where a small cluster of churches and other buildings mark the business centre of the town, which is one of the most popular of Thames resorts.

Sonning Cutting

Beyond Maidenhead, the view is interrupted in patches by cuttings, but not for long. The church steeple of SHOTTESBROOKE (6) appears on the left and marks an interesting 14th century building—one of the best in Berkshire. Through a gap between the cuttings a view opens out on the right to RUSCOMBE CHURCH (7), an interesting historical landmark in its way, for in a house which formerly stood opposite the church but has been demolished, the great William Penn, founder of Pennsylvania, died in 1718.

Beyond the next cutting the BATH ROAD (8) is seen drawing near

Ruscombe

to the railway again with its double line of telegraph poles. Like the railway, it soon passes through the village of TWYFORD (9), which in the early 19th-century aspired to becoming a centre of the silk-weaving industry, and a mill was established for that purpose, but the enterprise died out thirty years later.

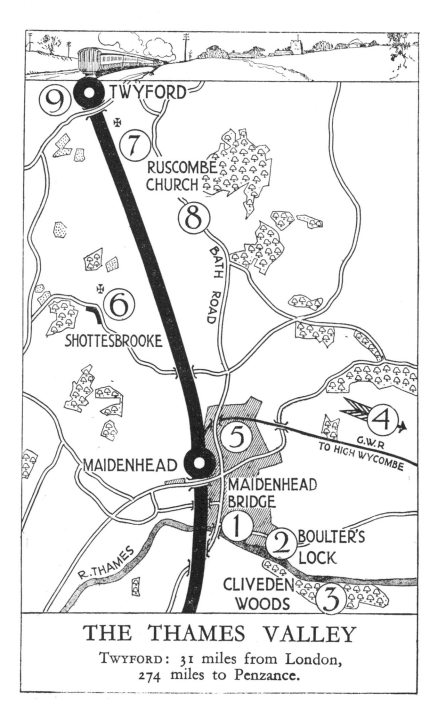

9 ⊙ TWYFORD

7

RUSCOMBE
CHURCH

8

BATH ROAD

6

SHOTTESBROOKE

4

G.W.R.
TO HIGH WYCOMBE

5

MAIDENHEAD

MAIDENHEAD
BRIDGE

1

2 BOULTER'S
LOCK

R. THAMES

CLIVEDEN
WOODS

3

THE THAMES VALLEY

TWYFORD: 31 miles from London,
274 miles to Penzance.

TWYFORD TO READING

The Thames

AT TWYFORD (1) the modern parish church is seen close to the station. The village is a large one, astride the London-to-Bath Road and was the scene, in 1688, of an encounter between those now almost forgotten antagonists — the Jacobites, and the partisans of William of Orange. From the station a branch curves off to the right for HENLEY-ON-THAMES (2), the famous regatta town lying about four miles north-west. The winding RIVER LODDON (3), which rises away to the left in Hampshire, flows under the railway and has only another couple of miles to travel before joining the Thames at WARGRAVE (4), towards which pretty village we have a view on the right, with the Chiltern Hills in the background.

We are still travelling through the quiet pastoral landscape of the Thames Valley and are rapidly approaching another bend of the river. On the left, adjoining the railway, is an extensive poultry farm maintained by one of the big poultry-food firms, and thousands of spic-and-span birds, mostly white, are seen grouped in the wired runs. On this side the landscape gradually rises towards the wooded country of the Hampshire border round about WOKINGHAM (5), belonging to the same great timber-belt as Windsor Forest.

Caversham House

On the opposite side, where the RIVER THAMES (6) is now only a mile away, a view is gained of the delightful riverside village of SONNING (7) with the Sonning GOLF COURSE (8) set close to the railway. Now the river sweeps into full view again and makes the foreground of a charming picture, with the imposing pile of CAVERSHAM HOUSE (9) standing on the higher ground of the opposite bank. This great mansion, formerly the seat of the Crawshay family, is a modern building occupying the site of earlier houses of historic interest, one of which was destroyed by fire, and another badly battered during the Civil Wars. Caversham House is now a Roman Catholic seminary.

The banks of the Thames are lined in characteristic English fashion by single rows of willow trees with stumpy bowls and

Caversham Bridge

branches that overhang the water, and the river comes right up to the railway. Here we are at the outskirts of READING (10). The name of the town is written in enormous white letters laid out flat in a grass field to the right as a mark for airmen. The RIVER KENNET (11), is crossed at the entrance to the town.

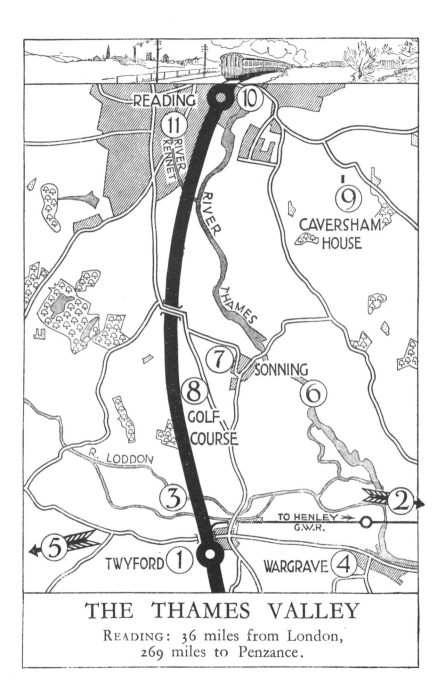

THE THAMES VALLEY

READING: 36 miles from London,
269 miles to Penzance.

MAIDENHEAD BRIDGE.

ROYAL BERKSHIRE

Reading and the Thames.   E. Margaret Holman.

ROYAL BERKSHIRE

IT would be an interesting thing to make a series of character studies of English counties, treating them as personalities. Where should we place Berkshire in such a category?

Berkshire is inclined to be shy and retiring, less often heard of in the newspapers than some of the more aggressive counties. She is beautiful, but in a modest, subtle way. The beauty of Westmorland is an obvious thing, seen at first glance; the beauty of Berkshire is a thing to be sought for and discovered. The search is fascinating and the end of it is satisfying, for Royal Berkshire holds a variety of beautiful scenery little suspected by those who only know the country around Windsor.

But we must give Windsor and its environs their due before passing on to other types of Berkshire landscape. Where Berkshire borders the Thames, the country is very much like that of "beautiful Bucks," with lush meadows and lovely woodlands bright with flowers in spring—a richly historical district with Windsor Castle as the chief focus-point of interest. The big industrial town of Reading, the charming resorts of Maidenhead, Twyford and other places through which the line passes, all belong to the Thames Valley aspect of Berkshire.

A different type of landscape lies further to the west, where gently undulating country marks the rise of that broad backbone of hills which stretches across country to the west for sixty miles or more—Berkshire Downs, Marlborough Downs, Salisbury Plain. It is, perhaps, not altogether easy to get the real " feeling " of this landscape from the train, for railways naturally follow the courses of the valleys, but it is at least possible to notice the contrast between Berkshire's undulations and the rather monotonously flat country nearer London. Of the valleys which break up the Berkshire Downs, the one with which we make the closest and longest acquaintance is that of the Kennet, through which we travel beyond Reading, and looking north from it towards the Lambourne Valley we have frequent impressions of the fine windswept uplands of Berkshire, with broad Commons, such as Bucklebury Common, which deserve to be as famous as the Surrey Commons although they have different characteristics. There is a fine sense of spaciousness and freedom about the uplands and much charming country on a small scale in the valleys, while some of the quaintest old towns and villages of England are to be found in Berkshire.

It is a great sportsman's county, too, for the Berkshire reaches of the Thames afford the best boating of any part of the river; Newbury has its racecourse, and the Downs up by Lambourne serve admirably as training grounds for the horses, while almost all the smaller Berkshire rivers offer excellent trouting.

READING TO THEALE

The Lion in Forbury Gardens

THE industrialism of READING (1) offers a sharp contrast to the green landscape in which the town is set. On the left great gas works are followed in quick succession by Huntley & Palmer's great biscuit factory and then the fortresslike building of the disused gaol in which Oscar Wilde was imprisoned. The FORBURY GARDENS (2) contain the huge Lion Monument to the men of the old 66th Regiment who fell in 1880. This "Maiwand Lion," as it is usually called, weighs 16 tons and is said to be the largest figure of a lion in existence. In these gardens are the remains of the once powerful Abbey of Reading, where a monk wrote one of the oldest of English popular songs, "Sumer is icumen in."

The tower on the left is that of ST. LAWRENCE'S CHURCH (3) dating from the 13th century. Now we fly through READING STATION (4), an important junction from which the big main lines to Swindon, Gloucester, Cheltenham, South Wales and other parts of the West Country go straight ahead, while we shape a course to the left into the Kennet Valley.

Southcott Manor

Close to the station on the right the magnificent new CAVERSHAM BRIDGE (5) opened in 1923, is seen crossing the Thames to Reading's residential suburb of CAVERSHAM (6), where smart red-roofed villas show up among trees on the rising ground. There is a glimpse also of Caversham Church, famous in pre-Reformation times for its wonderful collection of relics of saints.

Soon after passing through READING WEST STATION (7) we run clear of the town and turn almost due south until we are close to the RIVER KENNET (8), then bend to the west and run close alongside the stream for the next few miles.

On the right, just beyond where the BASINGSTOKE BRANCH (9) swerves off to the left, are the ruins of SOUTHCOTT MANOR HOUSE (10), a typical fifteenth-century mansion with a fine moat, which was the home of many generations of the Blagrave family and formerly boasted accommodation for 150 "horse and foot." Beyond the ruined manor house is seen PROSPECT PARK (11) and

Mill & Old House

Prospect House, now a public park. Soon we cross the HOLY BROOK (12), with a picturesque WATER MILL (13) and an old house with delightful gables and chimneys on the right, and the steeple of TILEHURST (14) a mile and a half across country. The village closer to the railway a little farther on is THEALE (15).

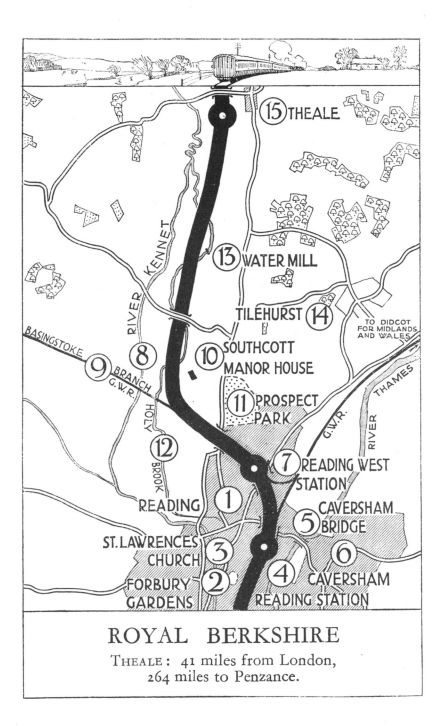

ROYAL BERKSHIRE

Theale: 41 miles from London,
264 miles to Penzance.

THEALE TO WOOLHAMPTON

Theale Church

THEALE CHURCH (1) shows up at the outskirts of the village to the right just after passing through the station. SULHAMPSTEAD HOUSE (2), which has been visible on the left for some little time, is the seat of Sir W. E. Watson, Bart., and beyond its park rises the church spire of SULHAMPSTEAD BANNISTER (3), while on the right are seen the grounds of ENGLEFIELD HOUSE (4), the seat of Mr. J. H. Benyon. This is a modern house looking very much like a castle, on the site of an older one which was for many years a seat of the Marquis of Winchester. The neighbouring spire is that of ENGLEFIELD CHURCH (5) in which lie many former owners of this ancient estate.

Two waterways keep the railway close company on the left. One of them, of course, is the RIVER KENNET (6), which serpentines through a landscape too flat to offer any resistance to its whims and fancies. In those bends lurk the wily trout which lure so many hopeful fishermen to this valley. They have the merit, too, of being picturesque, for a bargee would hardly consider the Kennet an ideal river for his trade, and so, long ago, the KENNET and AVON CANAL (7) was cut close alongside the river but making more of a bee-line from point to point. This canal, which connects the Severn with the Thames, sticks close to the Kennet for the next few miles and the railway frequently crosses both

Padworth House

Further along, on the left, is PADWORTH HOUSE (8), a former home of the Cowdrays and now the seat of Major C. W. Darby-Griffith, and in the background is a stretch of woodland through which we may let imagination travel to the Romano-British city of SILCHESTER (9), which lies in extensive ruin four miles from the railway. No Roman city of Britain has been so thoroughly excavated as Silchester, and Reading Museum is rich in specimens of Roman art from this site, where the amphitheatre, the forum, a Christian church, and a temple and many smaller buildings have been traced out.

On the right BEENHAM HOUSE (10), shows up in its spreading park, and the great Bath road comes close alongside. The

Woolhampton

country becomes more undulating. Beyond ALDERMASTON STATION (11), the fine park of ALDERMASTON COURT (12) shows up on the left near ALDERMASTON village, while at WOOLHAMPTON (13) the train crosses the village street on the level, giving a momentary peep of a typical rural scene.

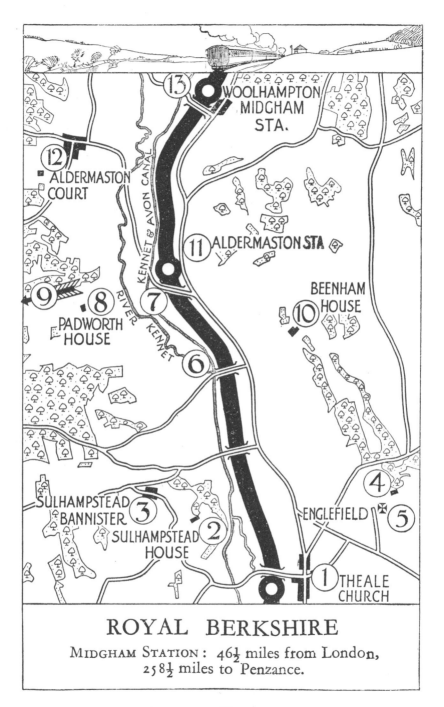

ROYAL BERKSHIRE

MIDGHAM STATION : $46\frac{1}{2}$ miles from London,
$258\frac{1}{2}$ miles to Penzance.

WOOLHAMPTON TO NEWBURY

Kennet Valley.

JUST north of Woolhampton village is DOUAI ABBEY (1), a modern Benedictine monastery and college named, of course, after the French town which became famous for its great college for English Roman Catholics. One of the most ancient crafts—basket-making—is represented by the osier beds which occupy the meadows of the Kennet banks close alongside the railway.

The church spire of BRIMPTON (2) is seen a mile across country to the left, while on a small hill to the right, looking very Continental and picturesque in spite of its modern origin, is the steeple of MIDGHAM CHURCH (3). Patches of woodland in the same direction mark the approaches to BUCKLEBURY COMMON (4), a favourite objective for excursions over the gently rolling Berkshire Downs. At THATCHAM STATION (5) the Kennet and the Canal both flow close beside the line on the left. The large village of THATCHAM (6) lies the best part of a mile away sprawling itself out in a long line upon the Bath Road. The name is a good one, for old thatched cottages have now become part and parcel of the landscape. "Thatch 'em" is a piece of good advice more easily given than followed, for thatching is a dying craft and expert thatchers are becoming more rare every year. Thatcham was a place of some importance in the days of the Normans, who have left a doorway in their characteristic style to share with

Brimpton Church

later features in the architectural composition of its ancient church.

The rising ground to the left of us divides the Kennet Valley from that of the River Enborne which runs almost parallel about a couple of miles away, and the large modern house seen on a hill with a fringe of woodland is ESSART (7), the residence of Mr. William Leng. Beyond it GREENHAM COMMON (8) spreads itself over the landscape, taking its name from the neighbouring village of GREENHAM (9) whose modern church shortly comes into view. The large house between Essart and Greenham village is GREENHAM LODGE (10), Mr. L. H. Baxendale's residence.

Now the line runs close alongside NEWBURY RACECOURSE (11), one of the best in the country and one of the most popular. It

Thatcham Church

was laid out by John Porter and opened in 1905. The full circuit is nearly two miles and there is a splendid straight mile 105 feet wide. The great stands are set close to NEWBURY RACE COURSE STATION (12). And now we reach the quaint old Berkshire town of NEWBURY (13).

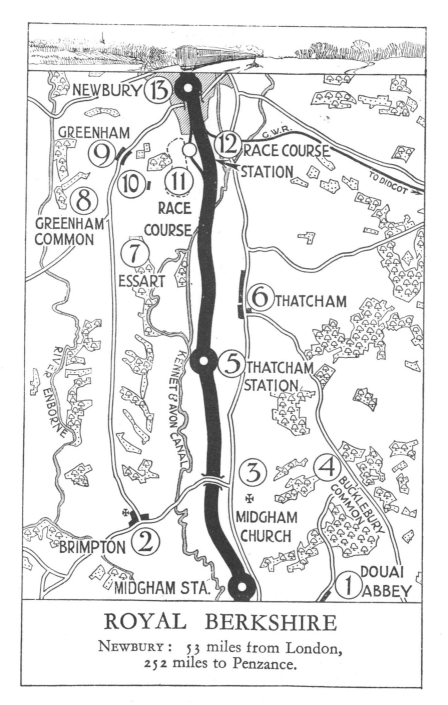

ROYAL BERKSHIRE

NEWBURY : 53 miles from London,
252 miles to Penzance.

NEWBURY TO HUNGERFORD

Newbury battlefield

WHO has not heard of "Jack of Newbury," one of the richest men in Tudor England, who lived in a fine mansion in NEWBURY **(1)** on a fortune made from the cloth trade. The Downs around the town have carried large flocks of sheep from time immemorial and a big wool fair is still held at Newbury each summer. Historically the place is famous for the two battles fought here during the Civil War. The site of the first BATTLE OF NEWBURY **(2)** lies about a mile across country to the left. The second battle was fought near SPEEN **(3)**.

This is a fascinating locality and we must try in hurried fashion to take our bearings. Newbury lies at the junction of the Kennet Valley with that of the tributary RIVER LAMBOURN **(4)** which comes down from the great open Downs to the north-west used as training grounds for race-horses. The country to the right of us belongs to Berkshire, but on the left the HAMPSHIRE DOWNS **(5)** are seen, the boundary between the two counties following the line of the RIVER ENBORNE **(6)**, which still flows parallel with the Kennet at a respectful distance.

The Tumulus

Through patches of woodland between the Lambourn and the Kennet to the right of us runs the straight track of a Roman road, the ERMINE STREET **(7)**, or, more strictly speaking, one of the Ermine Streets, for there is another which runs due north from London. The one we are concerned with here led across the hills to Gloucester. BENHAM HOUSE **(8)**, the seat of Sir Richard Sutton, on the right, came into prominence in March, 1923, on account of a daring theft of Gainsborough paintings from the mansion.

On the left, HAMSTEAD PARK **(9)**, a seat of the Earl of Craven, spreads itself over a square mile of country, and at the western extent of it, close to the railway, is a large prehistoric BURIAL MOUND **(10)**, or tumulus, planted with trees. HAMSTEAD MARSHALL CHURCH **(11)** is seen behind this great artificial mound. The landscape is full of winding streams forming a complicated network, and it is well-wooded too. KINTBURY **(12)**, was a

Kintbury

market town in ancient times. Close to its picturesque church on the left is a Saxon cemetery. AVINGTON **(13)**, to the right has a tiny Norman church, and beyond here on the left is the finely timbered HUNGERFORD PARK **(14)**. The mansion occupies the site of one built by Queen Elizabeth.

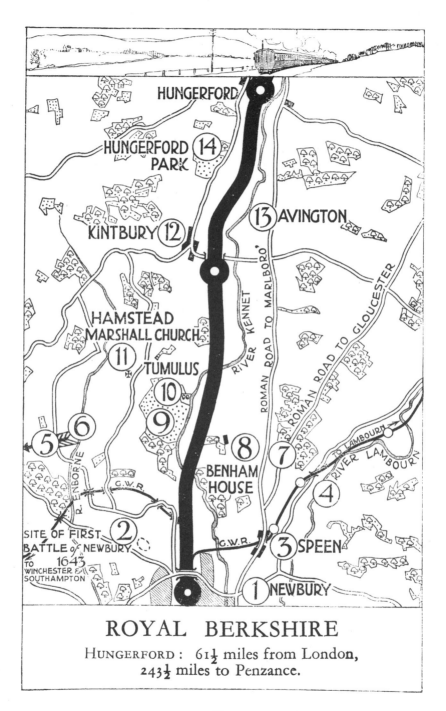

HUNGERFORD

HUNGERFORD PARK (14)

KINTBURY (12)

(13) AVINGTON

HAMSTEAD MARSHALL CHURCH

(11)

TUMULUS

(10)

(9)

(6)

(5)

RIVER KENNET

ROMAN ROAD TO MARLBORO'

ROMAN ROAD TO GLOUCESTER

TO LAMBOURN

RIVER LAMBOURN

(8)

(7)

(4)

BENHAM HOUSE

R. ENBORNE

G.W.R.

SITE OF FIRST BATTLE of NEWBURY
TO 1643
WINCHESTER &
SOUTHAMPTON

(2)

G.W.R.

(3) SPEEN

(1) NEWBURY

ROYAL BERKSHIRE

HUNGERFORD : $61\frac{1}{2}$ miles from London,
$243\frac{1}{2}$ miles to Penzance.

The Grand Avenue,
Savernake Forest.

MARLBOROUGH DOWNS

The Marlborough Downs.   H. G. Powell.

MARLBOROUGH DOWNS

TO label one stage of our journey " Marlborough Downs " and the next " Salisbury Plain " is admittedly to adopt a more or less arbitrary division for the sake of convenience. As a matter of fact both belong to a continuous stretch of country of almost uniform type, although not lacking in local variations. This great range of rolling hills rises superior to such artificial things as county boundaries and spreads over part of Berkshire, most of Wiltshire and a little way into both Hampshire and Dorset.

For part of the journey the Downs and the Plain keep us company simultaneously, the one on the right, the other on the left. The first stretch of country of this type to come into view belongs to Marlborough Downs ; the last we see of it before passing on into Somerset belongs to the main stock of Salisbury Plain.

Marlborough Downs have some points of difference underlying their family likeness to the wider expanse of Salisbury Plain, and one of these is the beautiful Savernake Forest, all the more precious because there is so little woodland in this part of England. The trees of the Forest are chiefly oak and beech, forming lovely glades where the roads pass through. The Forest is not a large one, being no more than sixteen miles in circumference, but its Grand Avenue forms one of the most beautiful stretches of main road in England. We have a good view of the Forest from the train and pass through the station which bears its name.

The Downs take their name from the old town of Marlborough which is set in the midst of them on the line of the great Bath Road close to where the River Kennet, of which we see a good deal, takes its rise among the hills. The foundation of the famous public school, Marlborough College, has a close connection with railway history, for it was established in the stately building of a fine old coaching inn, the " Castle," which had just retired from business in consequence of the Great Western Railway having opened a line to Marlborough. Marlborough lies about five miles north from the main line on which we travel, our nearest approaches to it being at Froxfield and Savernake.

Marlborough Downs, like Salisbury Plain, are liberally sprinkled with evidences of prehistoric life. Upon them lies the great Avebury Circle, of which the old antiquary Aubrey declares that it " as much surpasses Stonehenge as a cathedral does a parish church." The stones here are unhewn, and this fact points to the Avebury Circle being older than Stonehenge. Close to Avebury also is that astonishing monument, Silbury Hill, the largest artificial mound in Europe, which has so far defied all attempts to determine either its age or its purpose.

HUNGERFORD TO BEDWYN

Somerset Hospital

THE ancient market town of HUNGER-FORD (1) is in some sense a sister-town to Newbury, although much smaller. They lie less than eight miles apart and one gets into the habit of always thinking of them together for they both stand astride the Bath Road and share the same antique character. Hungerford, however, has also a reputation of its own as a trout-fishing centre. It has been that for centuries, and " trout farming," if not exactly the staple industry of the district, is at least a very important and interesting one. The Berkshire Trout Farm, with its succession of tanks for the young fry at various stages of development, is noticed on the right alongside the railway.

Just beyond Hungerford we cross the boundary into Wiltshire and at the same time bid farewell to the Kennet Valley. The RIVER KENNET (2) now flows to the right of the railway and we gradually get farther away from it, but the KENNET AND AVON CANAL (3) still keeps us close company. The Bath Road is also alongside on the right for a couple of miles beyond Hungerford, but we see the last of it at FROXFIELD (4), from which place it travels due west through Savernake Forest to Marlborough, while our own course bends to the south. A highly picturesque building which shows up finely at Froxfield is the SOMERSET HOSPITAL (5) which is a hospital in the original meaning of the

Chisbury Hill

term—a place of hospitality, or almshouse. This fine old building was founded in 1686 by Sarah, Duchess of Somerset, as a home for poor widows.

LITTLE BEDWYN (6) with its 13th century church lies beneath the shadow of CHISBURY HILL (7) which presents us with one of the most typical examples of a prehistoric hill-fortress that we shall see on this journey, although the countryside for a long stretch now is dotted with these memorials of our remote forefathers. The camp is an oval one, with earthwork walls standing 45 feet high—magnificent ! Moreover, it is not an isolated refuge but stands on the line of a great earthwork called the Wansdyke which ran across a long stretch of south-eastern England. The

Gt. Bedwyn

railway cuts across it here. On Chisbury Hill stands a little ruined CHAPEL OF ST. MARTIN (8) in the Decorated style of Gothic architecture.

The village of GREAT BEDWYN (9) stands close to the railway on the right. The church is seen on the right after passing through BEDWYN STATION (10).

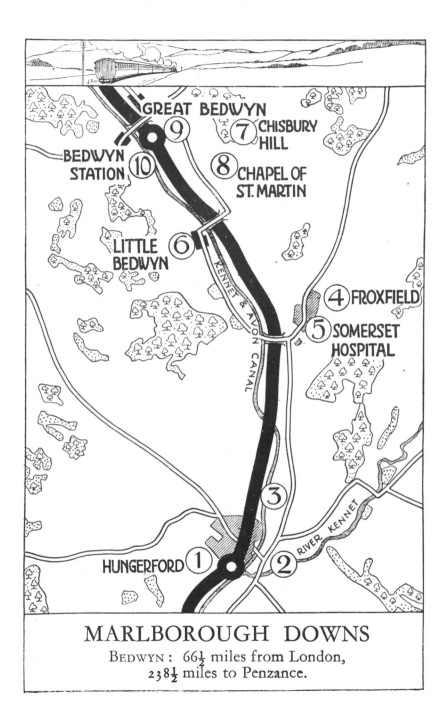

MARLBOROUGH DOWNS
BEDWYN: 66½ miles from London,
238½ miles to Penzance.

BEDWYN TO SAVERNAKE

Roman Road to Savernake

THE osier plantations of a few miles back have given place now to watercress beds in the little streams on either side of the line. Patches of woodland dotted about the landscape to right and left are detached members of the once extensive SAVERNAKE FOREST (1), the main surviving stock of which now lies two or three miles to the west. CHISBURY WOOD (2) sloping away to the south-west from Chisbury Hill is one of the larger of the detached fragments. The KENNET and AVON CANAL (3) is close alongside us on the left and gradually climbs the rising ground by a succession of locks at short intervals.

A mile and a half from Bedwyn Station the railway crosses the ROMAN ROAD (4) from Winchester to Cirencester. Its characteristically straight course is well defined on the right by an avenue of trees and it cuts right across the middle of TOTTENHAM PARK (5). Before making its exit from the Park, this ancient road develops into the GRAND AVENUE (6), one of the most famous and attractive features of Savernake Forest. Tottenham Park, the seat of Lord

Wolf Hall

Aylesbury, is really part and parcel of the Forest. The mansion stands in the middle of it, a little to the west of the Roman Road.

Another mansion, with rather more history attached to it, is WOLF HALL (7) which is seen on the left less than half a mile from the railway. The estate, formerly known as Wulfall, can be identified in Domesday Book and in the sixteenth century it was the home of Sir John Seymour, whose daughter Jane became the third wife of Henry VIII. and mother of Edward VI. The amorous Henry is said to have frequently visited Wolf Hall, but of the building in which this particular chapter of his courtships had its location very little now remains.

We are now travelling through the rolling country typical of the Marlborough Downs. The old town which gives its name to the landscape lies four miles across country to the right at the north-west extremity of Savernake Forest. The Kennet and Avon Canal disappears from view into a long TUNNEL (8) immediately to the left of the railway just before we reach SAVERNAKE STATION

Canal Tunnel

(9) and diving underneath the line duly issues forth on the right. The tunnel arch bears an inscription in honour of Thomas Bruce, Lord Aylesbury, and his son Charles, who were largely instrumental in carrying through the scheme for this canal, which was opened for traffic in 1810.

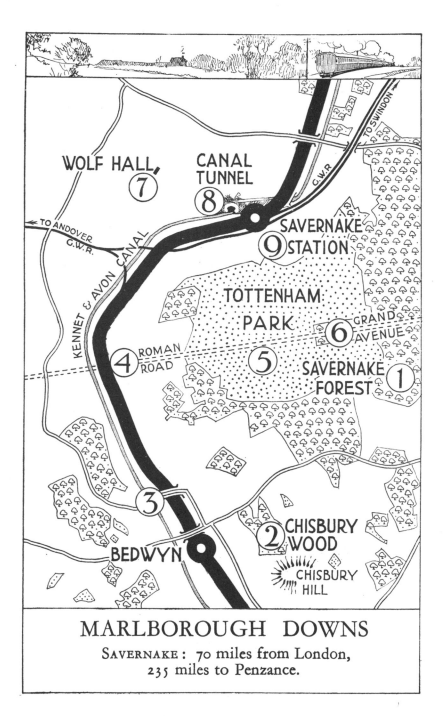

WOLF HALL,
⑦

CANAL
TUNNEL
⑧

TO SWINDON

G.W.R.

← TO ANDOVER
G.W.R.

KENNET & AVON CANAL

SAVERNAKE
⑨ STATION

TOTTENHAM
PARK

GRAND
⑥ AVENUE

ROMAN
④ ROAD

⑤

SAVERNAKE
FOREST ①

③

BEDWYN

②CHISBURY
WOOD

CHISBURY
HILL

MARLBOROUGH DOWNS

SAVERNAKE : 70 miles from London,
235 miles to Penzance.

SAVERNAKE TO PEWSEY

Martinsell Hill

THE chief mass of SAVERNAKE FOREST **(1)** is only half a mile away to the right of us now. A fine old house with tile-hanging decoration is noticed on the right soon after passing Savernake Station, but the chief landmark hereabouts, on the same side looking ahead, is MARTINSELL HILL **(2)**, the summit of which is crowned by a large prehistoric camp covering more than 30 acres. The hill rises 947 feet high and commands fine views across SALISBURY PLAIN **(3)** which now appears on the left—a long panorama of chalk downs stretching away from here to the borders of Hampshire, with the great temple of STONEHENGE **(4)** set, out of range, unfortunately, somewhere in the middle distance not very far from where Salisbury Cathedral raises its lovely spire as a landmark for many miles around. The rolling chalk hills are sprinkled with burial-mounds (tumuli).

The village of WOOTTON RIVERS **(5)** with an old church keeping close company with a collection of barns and farm buildings, lies near to the railway on the right as we gradually draw alongside

Edge of Salisbury Plain

Martinsell Hill, on which, by the way, are ancient pit-dwellings and tumuli as well as the large encampment already mentioned. Across country to the left, almost opposite Wootton Rivers, is EASTON HILL **(6)** on which are the traces of a British village.

A mile beyond Wootton Rivers we are at our nearest point to Martinsell Hill and can now study its impressive contours in more detail. There is a wonderful grandeur and dignity about the gradual sweep upwards to the summit, and as we travel on the hill turns out to be much longer than first impressions would suggest—a long ridge, or hog's back, rather than a cone, or sugar-loaf.

PEWSEY **(7)** groups itself well on the left, with the 15th century tower of its otherwise 13th century church rising above the village. Watercress beds are seen close to the line on the right. Salisbury Plain continues to march with us on the left, the hillsides scored with " wrinkles " left on them by prehistoric man. Some of these long wavy lines mark terraces constructed to prevent

Pewsey

wolves from reaching the higher ground on which the villages were pitched.

On that side of Martinsell Hill which we see from Pewsey, is a spot traditionally known as the GIANT'S GRAVE **(8)**, by no means the only such spot in Wiltshire, while EARTHWORKS **(9)** extend along the ridge to westward.

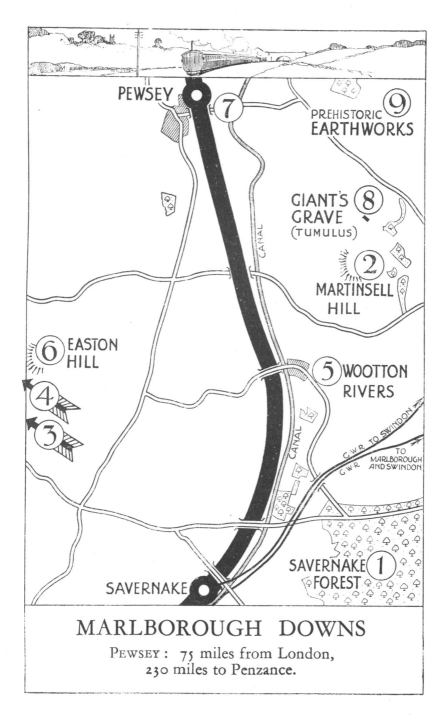

PEWSEY

⑦

PREHISTORIC
EARTHWORKS ⑨

GIANT'S ⑧
GRAVE
(TUMULUS)

②
MARTINSELL
HILL

CANAL

⑥ EASTON
HILL

⑤ WOOTTON
RIVERS

④

③

G.W.R. TO SWINDON

CANAL

G.W.R.
TO
MARLBOROUGH
AND SWINDON

SAVERNAKE

SAVERNAKE
FOREST ①

MARLBOROUGH DOWNS

PEWSEY: 75 miles from London,
230 miles to Penzance.

Stonehenge.

SALISBURY PLAIN

The White Horse, Westbury Hill   E. Margaret Holman

SALISBURY PLAIN

MARLBOROUGH DOWNS merge almost imperceptibly into the wider expanse of Salisbury Plain, where the landscape is modelled on a large pattern, and often runs unbroken for miles at a stretch in long, rounded contours that rise to considerable heights but never into sharp peaks. It is as though Nature for countless centuries had been rubbing away at a range of hills with a monstrous sheet of sandpaper, gradually obliterating their sharp points and minor indentations, leaving only the main lines of a vast design. The landscape is not without grandeur, but has little of the warm intimate charm of English scenery of the more kindly type. These wind-swept uplands can be very stern at times, as every traveller who has journeyed across them by road under varied weather conditions knows to his discomfort.

But from the vantage point of a comfortable seat in the Cornish Riviera Express the traveller feels nothing of the rigours of the landscape and is free to yield himself to its fascination. And the fascination of Salisbury Plain is something extraordinary. For these rolling downs that sweep away on our left are the cradle of the race, the oldest inhabited part of Britain, and the Englishman who can pass by without feeling any stirring of the blood, any quickening of the historic sense in him, may write himself down as a very dull fellow. It is true that the railway does not give us a glimpse of the mystic temple of Stonehenge, but many a hill-top shows the unmistakable lines of an ancient British camp, and lower down in many cases may still be seen the terrace which marks the line of defence against the wolves which roamed over Britain.

Ancient trackways used by our Celtic ancestors long before the Romans came can still be traced across the landscape, which is more thickly strewn here than in any other part of England with burial mounds, or tumuli, which have told us most of what is known of life in Britain away back in the mists and darkness of antiquity. Let us make a paradox and say that Salisbury Plain is a prehistoric history book.

Skirting the edge of the Plain as we do on this journey, it is seen neither at its best nor at its worst. Its chief archæological treasures and its most forbidding expanses of featureless country lie away from the railway track, but a number of points of real interest present themselves in succession—the White Horses of Milk Hill and Westbury, the great earthworks of Rybury Camp and Bratton Castle, the Giant's Grave and Adam's Grave, all with wonderful traditions to balance the scarcity of real history, while many a church of mediæval architecture helps to bridge the gulf between the present and the most distant past.

PEWSEY TO PATNEY

Woodborough

BEAUTIFUL twin hills, one of them with a sharp peak, are now seen on the right. These are PICKED HILL (1) and WOODBOROUGH HILL (2) rising 662 and 671 feet respectively. To the west of Woodborough Hill, the extremely ancient RIDGE WAY (3) runs on its almost straight course across country, where it may be traced for many miles. Due north from here, slightly over six miles distant, lies AVEBURY (4), one of the most fascinating places in Britain, for here stand at spacious intervals scores of huge stones which form a design far larger than that of Stonehenge. The vast circles of a temple and the great processional way leading to it are clear for all to see, and in the presence of these great monuments of a vanished race one is conscious of a sensation of awe not less than that felt on entering a great cathedral.

We may well travel this part of our journey in that spirit, for all around are the works of men whose ideas, however crude, were at least on a grand scale. Midway between us and Avebury the great earthwork called the WANS-DYKE (5), with which we have previously made acquaintance runs across country from east to west, over hillsides scored everywhere by smaller earthworks and so thickly dotted with tumuli as to form a vast cemetery many miles in extent.

Milk Hill & White Horse

On MILK HILL (6) is one of the most striking landmarks seen on this journey—a gigantic figure of a WHITE HORSE (7) cut in the hillside. This horse dates only from 1812 but some of the other white horses of this part of England, such as the one at Westbury which we shall see in a few minutes, are of extremely ancient origin. They are all described and illustrated and their situations clearly marked in an interesting little book* published by the Great Western Railway. The Milk Hill horse is 165 feet long and covers 700 square yards. It was formed by cutting away the turf and exposing the chalk of which the hill is composed.

Just below the horse is ADAM'S GRAVE (8), the subject of legend, like the Giant's Grave on Martinsell Hill. WOODBOROUGH (9)

Beechingstoke

is a prosperous village engaged in the manufacture of chemical fertilizers, The ancient earthwork of RYBURY CAMP (10), shows up on the right, and SALISBURY PLAIN (11) fills the picture to the left, where the village of BEECHINGSTOKE (12) is set in the foreground before reaching the station of PATNEY AND CHIRTON (13).

* "The White Horses of Wessex," price 6d.

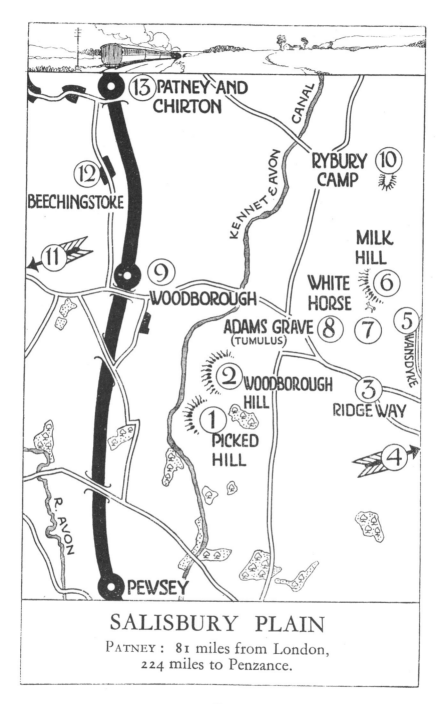

① PICKED HILL
② WOODBOROUGH HILL
③ RIDGEWAY
④
⑤ WANSDYKE
⑥ MILK HILL
⑦
⑧ ADAMS GRAVE (TUMULUS)
⑨ WOODBOROUGH
⑩ RYBURY CAMP
⑪
⑫ BEECHINGSTOKE
⑬ PATNEY AND CHIRTON

WHITE HORSE

KENNET & AVON CANAL

R. AVON

PEWSEY

SALISBURY PLAIN

PATNEY : 81 miles from London,
224 miles to Penzance.

43

PATNEY TO EDINGTON

Stert & Etchilhampton Hill

RYBURY CAMP (1) ranges itself away to the right on the summit of Clifford's Hill, a spur of ST. ANNE'S HILL (2) which rises to a height of 900 feet and is the highest point of the Marlborough Downs. A long-established fair, which draws folk from all the scattered villages and isolated farmsteads of the surrounding countryside, is held on St. Anne's Hill in August each year, and by a quaint corruption of the name, is known as Tan Hill Fair. Rybury Camp is an earthwork probably of Celtic origin.

About a couple of miles beyond Patney, the main road from Salisbury to Devizes, the ancient county town of Wiltshire, crosses over the railway just beyond the point at which the branch line to Devizes bears off to the right, and the village of STERT (3) with its church is seen in the angle between the two railways. Behind it rises the rounded form of ETCHILHAMPTON HILL (4), 626 feet high.

DEVIZES (5), although out of sight, lies only a couple of miles across country beyond Stert. It is a dignified old place with a rich history, but being an isolated town between the thinly populated areas of the Marlborough Downs and Salisbury Plain, has been left in a quiet backwater by the stream of modern life. Roman household gods and coins have been found there, and fragmentary remains of its ancient castle still exist.

Salisbury Plain

A broad valley opens up a long unbroken view to the right, and as the line bends south-west BLOUNT'S COURT (6), a modern castellated house, comes into view on the right. Behind it is POTTERNE (7) one of many beautiful villages, marked by old thatched cottages, which lie dotted about the spreading Plain. On the left, the small PARHAM WOOD (8) and other patches of timber break the almost treeless expanse of downland. At LAVINGTON STATION (9) another main road from Salisbury to Devizes passes under the railway.

On the left, marked out by the squat tower of its church, now appears the village of GREAT CHEVERELL (10), backed by the woods of ERLESTOKE PARK (11), while in the same direction the long line of Salisbury Plain forms the horizon. COULSTON HILL (12) and STOKE HILL (13), rising to a height of 729 feet, are seen as a background to the village of EAST COULSTON (14), while a little farther along on the same side EDINGTON HILL (15) rises to a height of 666 feet just behind the village of that name.

Great Cheverell

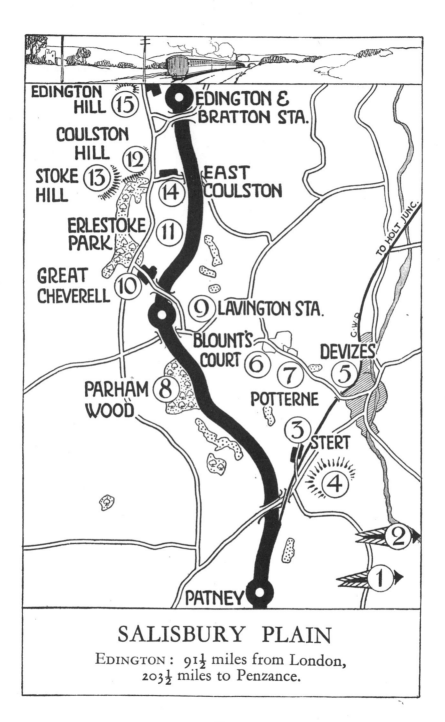

SALISBURY PLAIN

EDINGTON : 91½ miles from London,
203½ miles to Penzance.

EDINGTON TO WESTBURY

Edington Priory Ch.

THE next few miles of the journey are crowded with varied interest. Passing through EDINGTON & BRATTON STATION (1) the large village of EDINGTON (2) with a beautiful Priory Church is seen on the left. This splendid specimen of 14th century architecture was built by a native of the place, William de Edyndune, who became Bishop of Winchester and began that important re-building of Winchester Cathedral, which was completed by his more famous successor, William of Wykeham. EDINGTON HILL (3) still shows up well behind the village.

The next hill, rising to a height of 754 feet, is WESTBURY HILL (4) which bears on its summit the great earthwork called BRATTON CASTLE (5) with fine trenches clearly marked by the long ridges on the hillside. Possibly this earthwork was originally formed in prehistoric times, but, however that may be, tradition asserts that it was to this spot that the Danish king Guthrum retired after suffering heavy defeat by the English hero Alfred the Great, at the battle of Ethandune in 878.

Westbury Hill juts out prominently from the main line of Salisbury Plain at this point and as we travel alongside it and are able to view its western slopes another famous landmark comes into view. This is the WESTBURY WHITE HORSE (6), a most distinguished member of the large family of Wessex white

White Horse Hill & Bratton Castle

horses with which we have previously made acquaintance, in the person of one of its younger sons, at Milk Hill (see page 42). The Westbury White Horse is one of the hoary ancestors of the tribe and is undoubtedly of very early origin. Tradition declares that it was cut to commemorate King Alfred's great victory at Ethandune, to which allusion has just been made. Having become overgrown in places, it was re-cut in 1778 and received a further drastic grooming in 1873. It measures 175 feet from head to tail and stands 107 feet high (how many " hands " is that ?), and King Arthur could have set up his Round Table on the eye, which has a circumference of 25 feet.

On the right against a wooded background is seen Lord Ludlow's

Heywood House

seat, HEYWOOD HOUSE (7), the successor of a Jacobean mansion. Now the old town of WESTBURY (8) lies close ahead on the left, with railway plant works and cloth weaving and glove making industries with iron ore mining near the station. To the right just opposite the town, is the site of a BRITISH SETTLEMENT (9).

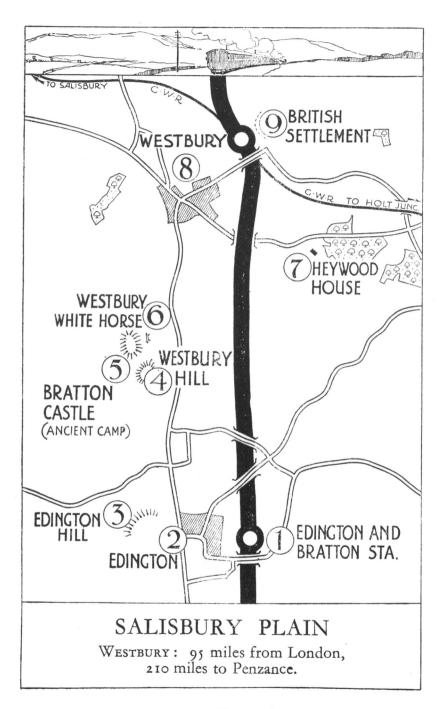

TO SALISBURY

G.W.R

WESTBURY

⑨ BRITISH SETTLEMENT

⑧

G.W.R TO HOLT JUNC.

⑦ HEYWOOD HOUSE

WESTBURY WHITE HORSE ⑥

⑤

⑧ WESTBURY HILL

BRATTON CASTLE (ANCIENT CAMP)

EDINGTON HILL ③

② EDINGTON

① EDINGTON AND BRATTON STA.

SALISBURY PLAIN

WESTBURY: 95 miles from London,
210 miles to Penzance.

WESTBURY TO FROME

The White Horse

AFTER crossing BISS BROOK (1), which develops into the River Biss which flows through Trowbridge four miles to the north, we have a view on the right of FAIRWOOD HOUSE (2), the seat of Sir John Hatchard; and at the point just beyond here where the line passes between two small patches of woodland the boundary is crossed from Wiltshire into Somerset.

Away to the left, looking across BLACK DOG WOOD (3) and some low intervening hills, the summit of CLEY HILL (4) is seen rising in the distance, about four miles due south. Like so many —one might almost say like most—of the prominent heights in this part of England it has a prehistoric camp at the summit. The hill rises to 800 feet and commands fine views. Historically, it is interesting as the site of one of the great beacon fires which gave warning of the approach of the Spanish Armada. Cley Hill marks within a mile or two the situation of the old Wiltshire town of Warminster. As we go forward we have a much better view of Cley Hill, as the foreground slopes away into the valley of the Frome. The trenches of the camp then show up very plainly.

Berkeley

The mansion which now comes into view on the right is STANDERWICK COURT (5), a building of the Queen Anne period, now the seat of Colonel Algernon Goff. The village church of BERKLEY (6) which lies to the left, close to the western end of Black Dog Wood is a most unexpected kind of building to be found in this out-of-the-way country place, for it has a dome in the Renaissance style of Sir Christopher Wren, copied direct from the well-known Wren church of St. Stephen, Walbrook, close to the Mansion House in London—Wren's experiment in dome construction before making his supreme venture at St. Paul's.

Now the busy old town of FROME (7) is seen a short distance ahead to the right of the railway, but before entering it we must cross the RIVER FROME (8), which is a tributary of that particular River Avon which flows through Bath. The name Frome, by the way, is pronounced Froom. The town has a population of

Frome

10,000 and is a market centre for a wide area. It has cloth factories, iron and bronze foundries and other industries, and from the midst of this commercial activity rises the steeple of the parish church, an ancient building restored in modern times, while the tower seen on higher ground is that of Christ Church.

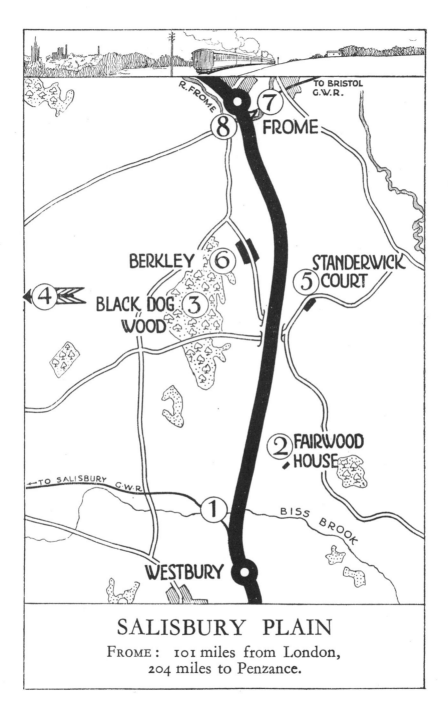

TO BRISTOL
G.W.R.

R. FROME

⑦

⑧ FROME

BERKLEY ⑥

④◄◄◄

BLACK DOG ③
WOOD

STANDERWICK
⑤ COURT

②FAIRWOOD
HOUSE

←TO SALISBURY G.W.R.

①

BISS BROOK

WESTBURY

SALISBURY PLAIN

Frome: 101 miles from London,
204 miles to Penzance.

THE WELLINGTON MONUMENT.

LOVELY
SOMERSET

Taunton

HAPowell

LOVELY SOMERSET

THE long succession of stern uncompromising contours which make up Salisbury Plain leaves us in a mood to appreciate something less severe, if also less dramatic. The Plain, magnificently barbaric, makes us think of Celts and Druids; the more kindly landscape of Somerset suggests dairy farming, creamy milk and fat cheeses. Villages occur more frequently and the harshness of bare hills gives place to woodland.

So much for the pleasant surface of things. Beneath it lies a story of violent upheaval and the play of natural forces on a scale almost unimaginable. Few parts of England have undergone more drastic changes of form and geography. At some remote period the sea washed right across the smiling landscape over which we travel. Places like Bruton and Castle Cary stood on the coast, from which they are now forty-five miles distant. Of the hills which now rise out of the landscape only the peaks were visible and they formed an archipelago of islets. Fossil sea shells are found in Somerset at five hundred feet above present sea-level.

And so, if we have lost the Land of Lyonesse by the encroachment of the sea on Cornwall, we have gained the fertile lands of Somerset, now redolent with memories of the great heroes of the race—the dim, legendary figure of King Arthur and the solid historical personality of Alfred the Great. King Arthur is closely connected by legend with Glastonbury and we may think of him when we come in sight of Glastonbury Tor. The Vale of Avalon in which he " came to his end " lies a little to the north of our course, but in Cadbury Camp we may see one of the places identified with Camelot, the scene of Arthur's brilliant court. It is in Somerset, according to legend, that King Arthur and his knights will re-appear to fight for England in her hour of greatest need.

With Alfred the Great we are on more certain ground. We shall pass through Athelney, where he burnt the cakes, and see the great White Horse of Westbury and Alfred's Tower, both commemorating his victory over the Danes in 878.

Another long stride through history brings us to the dominating figure of the Iron Duke, who took his title from the Somerset town of Wellington when the nation showered honours on him after the victory of Waterloo. His monument stands out finely upon the Blackdown Hills, one of three charming ranges which are outstanding features of the Somerset scenery.

The wonderful hill ranges of Somersetshire are in view at various parts of the journey. The Quantocks stand out against the sky-line north of Taunton and there is a view of the beautiful Mendips from Bruton, while the Blackdown Hills are seen at close range as we approach the border of Devon.

FROME TO WITHAM FRIARY

Cley Hill

CLEY HILL (1) keeps us company on the left for some time after passing Frome. The hill may be considered a western outpost of the Salisbury Plain country, and we now enter a different and more hospitable landscape.

The change is marked almost at once by the fine mass of woodland around LONGLEAT HOUSE (2), one of the " stately homes of England " and the historic seat of the Marquis of Bath. The house stands close beside a beautiful lake in a widespread Deer Park, hidden from view by the beautiful LONGLEAT WOODS (3), part of a vast area of woodland stretching in a broad irregular band six miles across country to the east and six miles south-west from the point at which we make our first acquaintance with it.

At this north-west corner of the woods stands the small village of SELWOOD (4) marked by the modern church steeple seen rising amid trees on its hill site. On the right appears MARSTON HOUSE (5), an ancient seat of the Earls of Cork and Orrery, rebuilt in 1857, and now the residence of Mr. and Mrs. Bonham Carter.

In the distance, nearly six miles away, close to the line of a Roman road which we shall shortly cross, is seen CRANMORE TOWER (6), on a hill 928 feet high, adjoining Cranmore House, the seat of Sir R. Paget. The tower, built in 1862, is what the Italians would call a "belvedere," constructed for the luxurious

Longleat

purpose of enabling wider views to be obtained than those seen from the house itself. It stands out very prominently, looking from the distance like a tall pillar.

POSTLEBURY WOOD (7) spreads a fine mantle over Postlebury Hill, and just beyond here is the track of the old ROMAN ROAD (8) which cuts across country in a straight line for Bath.

Above the woods on the left the little church of GAER HILL (9) is seen on the sky-line. These woodlands, a continuation of Longleat Woods, form WITHAM PARK (10), while close to the railway on the right just before passing through the station of WITHAM FRIARY (11) is seen the ancient church with an apse and quaint little bell-turret, which represents all that is left of a Carthusian monastery founded here in 1181.

Witham Church

Beyond Witham Park on the left is seen the stretch of woodland called KINGSWOOD WARREN (12), and above this rises very prominently on the summit of a hill ALFRED'S TOWER (13), 150 feet high commemorating King Alfred's great victory over the Danes.

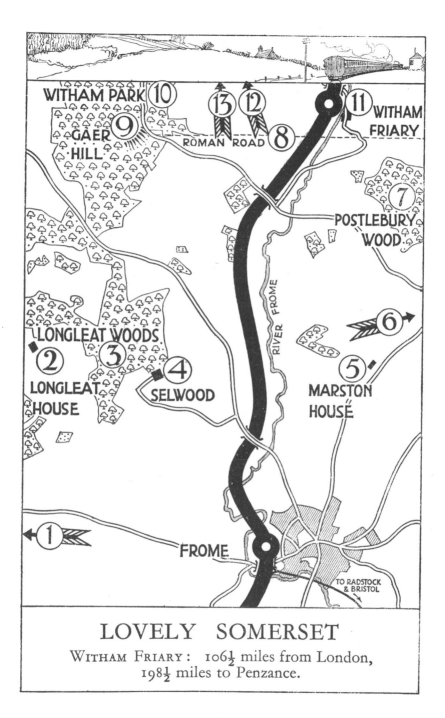

LOVELY SOMERSET

WITHAM FRIARY: $106\frac{1}{2}$ miles from London,
$198\frac{1}{2}$ miles to Penzance.

WITHAM FRIARY TO CASTLE CARY

Alfred's Tower

THE village of UPTON NOBLE (1) now lies on the right, with no more than the saddle-back roof of its small church visible above the surrounding houses. A mile farther on, however, an interesting little building stands close to the railway on the same side. This is an ancient RUINED CHAPEL (2) at Batt's Farm. At least it is usually called a chapel but is much more likely to have been a mediæval tithe-barn. Just beyond is PINK WOOD (3).

ALFRED'S TOWER (4) still shows up prominently on its wooded hill to the left, and we are rather closer to it now. The country through which we are passing is rich in memories of the great Saxon king. The great victory which the Westbury White Horse and this tower both commemorate was probably gained at Edington in Wiltshire, through which we have lately passed, but the peace which followed was made at Wedmore in Somerset, which now lies about fifteen miles to the north of us.

The little RIVER BRUE (5) now flows close beside the line on the left, along the edge of COGLEY WOOD (6), and in another mile is reached on the right the pretty little town of BRUTON (7) —"the Brue-town"—an ancient and interesting place. We have a glimpse of its fine Perpendicular church, the successor of one built by Bishop Aldhelm in 688. There was an Augustinian Abbey

Tithe Barn at Batt's Farm

here in mediæval times, and the monastic dove-cote is seen on the left immediately after passing through the station. (Sketch on page 56). Almost due north is seen CREECH HILL (8) which once served as a beacon and has a pre-historic camp on its summit (621 feet).

As the land on the right of us slopes gently down into the valley of the Brue and its tributary, the RIVER ALHAM (9) we have a view of the distant MENDIP HILLS (10), one of the most charming features of the Somerset scenery. It is a curiously isolated range, rising abruptly out of low-lying country, with beautiful glens and gorges dividing the uplands. Discoveries of animal remains in the numerous natural caves of the Mendips prove that these beautiful hills were the home of many wild animals, including the lion

Bruton

and the hyena, which have been extinct in Britain for scores of centuries. A wonderful collection of these remains is in Taunton Museum.

The ancient town of CASTLE CARY (11) now lies on the left, and at CASTLE CARY STATION (12) the main line to Yeovil, Dorchester and Weymouth turns off.

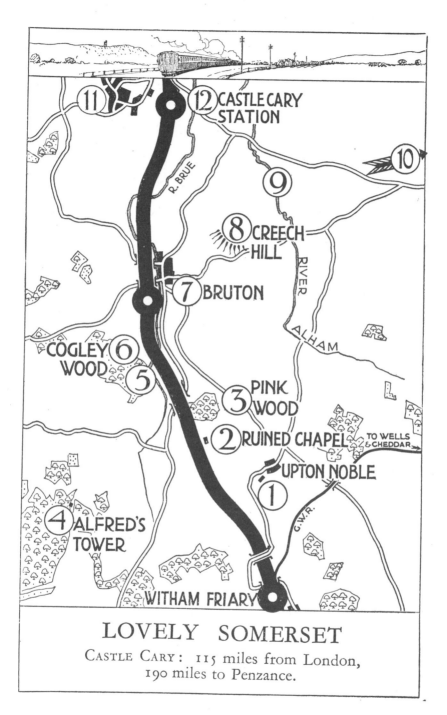

LOVELY SOMERSET

CASTLE CARY: 115 miles from London,
190 miles to Penzance.

CASTLE CARY TO CHARLTON MACKRELL

Dove Cote at Bruton

CASTLE CARY (1) is a small market town near the source of the RIVER CARY (2), which soon comes within a mile of the RIVER BRUE (3), as though to join it, then changes its mind and wanders off in another direction. Of the castle of Castle Cary only fragmentary remains exist. History says Charles II. slept here after the Battle of Worcester; it would be wiser perhaps to say that he tried to. The town is concerned with horse-hair weaving, and the spire of its church is seen on the left with ANSFORD CHURCH (4) nearer the railway.

A striking landmark eight miles distant on the right, looking west, is GLASTONBURY TOR (5), a prominent hill bearing on its summit the ruined chapel of St. Michael, once the resort of pilgrims to the shrine of St. Joseph of Arimathea at Glastonbury Abbey. Glastonbury was famous for its miraculous Holy Thorn. A beautiful legend tells how St. Joseph, coming here as a pilgrim, planted his staff in the earth while he knelt to pray; the hard staff burst into bud and became a living tree, which always blossomed on Christmas Day.

Half a mile from the railway on the right, ALFORD CHURCH (6) is set beside the River Brue, and we pass through ALFORD HALT (7). A little way beyond here the church tower of LOVINGTON (8) is seen on the left, and a little more than four miles across country in the same

Glastonbury Tor

direction appears CADBURY CASTLE (9), generally considered to be the " Camelot " of King Arthur's Court. Around the steep sides of the hill are four lines of earthworks and this camp is said to have been the last British stronghold in the West to hold out against the Romans. Many skeletons of men and boys discovered in a neighbouring field, buried quite haphazard, are believed to have been those of the last British defenders. Some Roman coins and one early British coin have been found on the hill, which seems to have formed the central stronghold of a larger defensive organisation, represented by smaller camps on neighbouring hills.

WHEATHILL CHURCH (10) stands close to the line on the left, and EAST LYDFORD CHURCH (11) on the right, with Glastonbury Tor still showing up finely in the distance.

Cadbury Camp (Camelot)

The village of KEINTON MANDEVILLE (12) has the honour of having been the birthplace of Sir Henry Irving, in 1838. PENNARD HILL (13), near Glastonbury, rises 400 feet on the right. On the left is the church tower of CHARLTON ADAM (14).

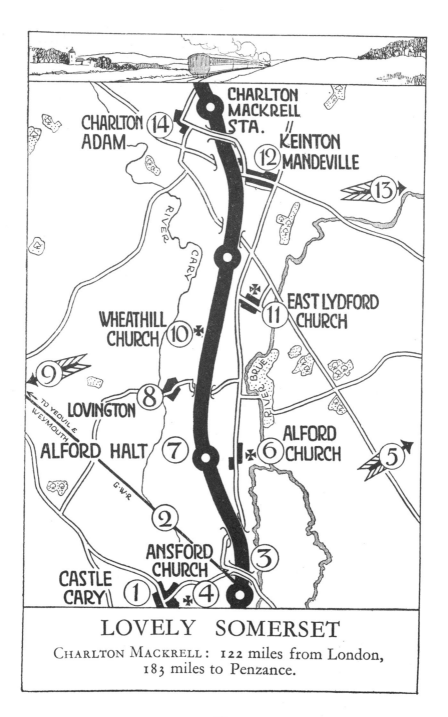

LOVELY SOMERSET

CHARLTON MACKRELL: 122 miles from London,
183 miles to Penzance.

CHARLTON MACKRELL TO LANGPORT

Charlton Mackrell

THE church of KINGWESTON (1) is seen on the right just before we pass through Charlton Mackrell. The name of CHARLTON MACKRELL (2), of which the church tower appears on the left but most of the village on the right, has a distinctly fishy sound about it, and there is something very appropriate in this, whatever the historical derivation may be, for in prehistoric days this district was covered either by the sea or by lagoons bordering the sea, and had lake villages built on piles. The idea of fishing for mackerel at Charlton Mackrell is by no means as absurd as it looks at first glance—just a question of time !

We will come back to this subject in a moment, but meanwhile attention is claimed by DUNDON HILL (3), a camp-crowned beacon 337 feet high which appears on the right beyond the broad expanse of Copley Wood. Just here the railway cuts right through the site of a ROMAN SETTLEMENT (4), of which earthworks and a paved road are still visible between the railway and Copley Wood.

On the left the sight of a picturesque church tower, partly octagonal, warns us that we are approaching SOMERTON (5). A place with such a name ought obviously to be the county town of Somerset, and as a matter of fact it formerly carried that dignity, long since wrested from it by historic, independent, busy, prosperous Taunton.

Dundon Hill

Somerton is a quaint little place with an ancient market cross and other picturesque old buildings. It stands on the RIVER CARY (6) which here flows under the railway, a much broader stream than when we first saw it. Along its course, towards Dundon Hill, the landscape becomes entirely flat and crossed by numerous dykes is like the Fens of Lincolnshire and Cambridgeshire—an obvious link with lake-village days. This particular stretch is called SOMERTON MOOR (7) but a little farther to north-west is Sedgemoor of historic memory.

SOMERTON TUNNEL (8), rather more than a thousand yards long, is the first since leaving London, which is now 126 miles distant. On emerging from it, LONG SUTTON CHURCH (9) appears on the left just before reaching the station of LONG SUTTON AND PITNEY (10).

Somerton Church

PITNEY church (11) appears on the right and on the left is seen MUCHELNEY CHURCH (12) concerning which the gruesome tale is told that the builder of the tower hanged himself on seeing the much finer tower built by his apprentice at HUISH EPISCOPI (13) which we pass just before reaching LANGPORT (14).

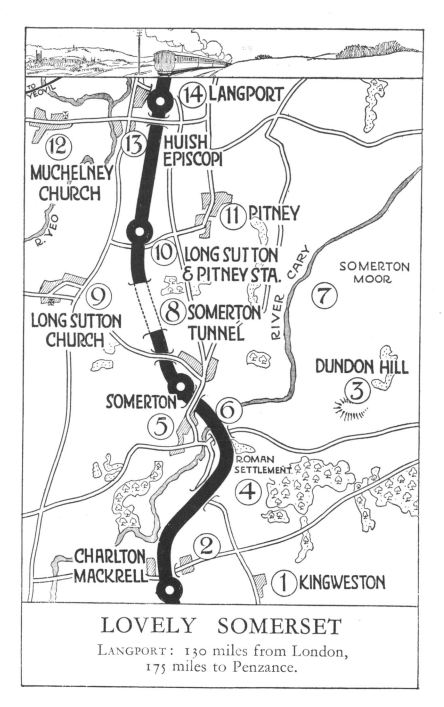

LOVELY SOMERSET

LANGPORT: 130 miles from London,
175 miles to Penzance.

59

LANGPORT TO ATHELNEY

Huish Episcopi

THE church tower of Huish Episcopi (1) is certainly of unusually beautiful proportions. The neighbouring church of Langport (2) which is also seen on the left is well known among students of ancient painted glass for its interesting fragments of that lovely branch of mediæval art. Langport is a small market town on the River Parrett (3), and its cattle market is noticed on the left close to the station.

Hills rise on either side of the railway here, but the valley of the Parrett broadens out into another expanse of low-lying country which still has a marshy character as it had in days far beyond the reach of written history. The stretch lying immediately ahead on the right is called Aller Moor (4), and looking across it we see, where the hills subside into the valley, the church and village of Aller (5) where Alfred the Great is said to have baptised—in the Saxon font still to be seen in Aller Church—the Danish leader Guthrum and many of his followers, shortly after the great Battle of Ethandune to which we have already had occasion to make more than one reference.

The remarkable way in which the land around here is drained by perfectly straight dykes running at right angles to each other and giving a strangely symmetrical character to the landscape as seen from above, will impress every observant traveller. It is very suggestive of the Fen country around the Wash.

Langport

Away to the right, beyond the villages of Othery (6) and Middlezoy (7), both of whose churches stand out above the general flatness, stretches Sedgemoor (8), the site of the famous battle which ended the Duke of Monmouth's rebellion in 1685, being about two miles north-east from Middlezoy.

The Polden Hills (9) are seen rising to modest heights beyond the level stretch of Sedgemoor, while to the left, on the higher ground bordering West Sedge Moor (10), which would be better termed South Sedgemoor, is seen the Parkfield Monument (11), 140 feet high, erected in 1768 by the Earl of Chatham to commemorate Sir William Pynsent. Also on the left, but at closer range, appears the church of Stoke St. Gregory (12). A mile and a half to the right is seen the great Burrowbridge Mound (13) traditionally identified as "King Alfred's Fort," and actually used as a fort during the Civil Wars. Athelney (14) is close to the junction of the River Tone (15) with the Parrett.

Parkfield Monument

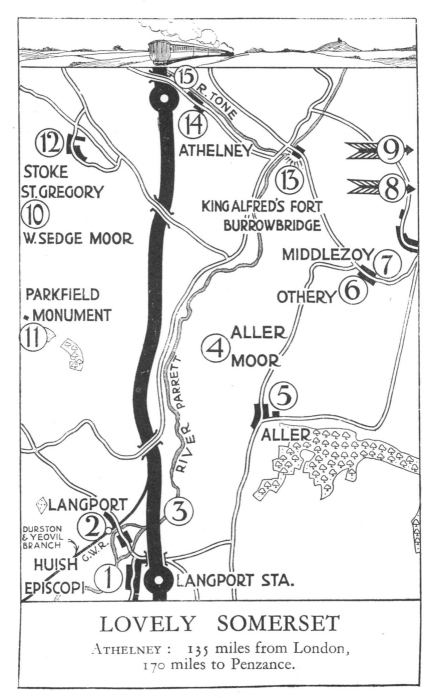

⑮
R. TONE

⑭
ATHELNEY

⑫ STOKE
ST.GREGORY
⑩
W.SEDGE MOOR

⑬
KING ALFRED'S FORT
BURROWBRIDGE

⑨

⑧

MIDDLEZOY **⑦**

OTHERY **⑥**

PARKFIELD
• MONUMENT
⑪

④ ALLER
MOOR

⑤

ALLER

RIVER PARRETT

◈LANGPORT
③

DURSTON
& YEOVIL
BRANCH
G.W.R.

②

HUISH
EPISCOPI

① LANGPORT STA.

LOVELY SOMERSET

ATHELNEY : 135 miles from London,
170 miles to Penzance.

ATHELNEY TO TAUNTON

Burrowbridge

WITH "King Alfred's Fort" on Burrow-bridge Mound still showing up on the right, we pass the ISLE OF ATHELNEY (1), the traditional location of the humble cottage in which the great leader of the English had his ears boxed for allowing the cakes to burn. Here in these marshes he found refuge and rest in preparation for his final and successful onslaught against the Danes. The Isle is a slight rise above the level of the flat lands; upon it in mediæval times stood an abbey, and now there is a pillar, erected in 1801, with an inscription commemorating the greatest English King.

Looking ahead to the right, a distant view is gained of the QUANTOCK HILLS (2), that lovely range of West Somerset stretched out in a panorama that contrasts strongly with the flat landscape closer at hand, in which osiers for basket-making are grown on a large scale. A little way beyond the Isle of Athelney is seen the village of LYNG (3) with its ancient church, while on the left, beyond the level stretch of CURRY MOOR (4), through which flows the RIVER TONE (5), is seen on slightly higher ground the village of NORTH CURRY (6), its venerable church showing a fine octagonal tower. In the distance on the same side are seen the Blackdown Hills, with which we shall soon make a closer acquaintance.

Lyng Church

The BRIDGWATER & TAUNTON CANAL (7) coming down from Bridgwater, which lies half a dozen miles to the north, runs alongside on the right for the next four miles, while the RIVER TONE (8) comes close up to us on the left at CREECH ST. MICHAEL (9) whose church is famous for an extremely ancient carving of the Holy Trinity over the west door. The neighbouring village of RUISHTON (10) also presents an ancient church with a fine tower, but all eyes are now set on the magnificent group of church towers straight ahead on the left which mark the county town of TAUNTON (11) which is entered just after crossing the Bridgwater and Taunton Canal.

Taunton is a fine town, with the dignity, if not the legal status, of a city. It has splendid architecture, as we may see even in

Creech St. Michael Church

this passing glimpse, with the noble tower of St. Mary's Church as the chief of a fine group of four. Taunton has a rich history, too, for its castle was founded in the eighth century by Ina, King of the West Saxons, and a large part of the mediæval building still remains.

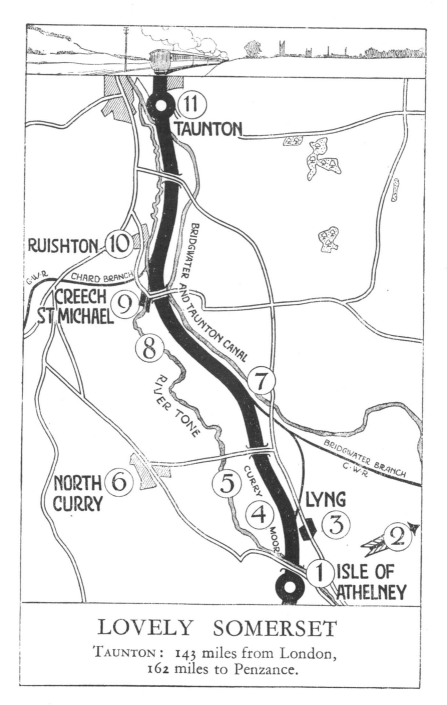

LOVELY SOMERSET

Taunton: 143 miles from London,
162 miles to Penzance.

TAUNTON TO WELLINGTON

Taunton

TAUNTON (1) figures largely in the Civil War period and later on was the place chosen by the Duke of Monmouth to proclaim himself king—an event which had its sequel in the Bloody Assize held here by Judge Jeffreys. It is now a thriving agricultural and silk-weaving centre with a population of 24,000.

No sooner are we clear of Taunton's houses and factories than a long view opens out on the left across to where the Blackdown Hills rise about a thousand feet and the Wellington obelisk is seen on the ridge even from this distance of seven or eight miles. We shall find ourselves at much closer quarters with the hills and the monument in a few minutes.

Meanwhile there are several points of interest to note in the lowlands nearer at hand. On the right is seen TAUNTON SCHOOL (2), a notable public school, situated at Staplegrove, on the road from Taunton to Milverton. The School opened its history in 1847 as the Independent College, a centre of education for boys from Nonconformist families. The buildings we now see, however, date from 1870.

Taunton School

The ancient octagonal church tower seen on the left is that of BISHOP'S HULL (3), more strictly Bishops Hull Without to distinguish it from Bishops Hull Within, which is one of the parishes of Taunton. The ancient parish of Bishops Hull stretched right to the centre of what is now Taunton and included Taunton Castle within its area.

Looking to the right again, the church of NORTON FITZWARREN (4) is seen, and with a pair of field glasses one might pick out some of the vigorously carved gargoyles which decorate its exterior. Local tradition declares that " dragons bred extensively in this parish," but the stud book of the Norton Fitzwarren dragon herd has yet to be discovered.

NORTON FITZWARREN STATION (5) is an important junction from which the branches to Minehead and Ilfracombe leave the main line. The church tower of BRADFORD (6) now shows up on the left. The village has the alternative name of Bradford-on-Tone, and has a beautiful bridge crossing the river. As the bridge

Norton Fitzwarren

dates from the 14th-century the days of the " ford " must be distant indeed. The BLACKDOWN HILLS (7) and the WELLINGTON MONUMENT (8) come closer into view as we travel south-west. The church tower of OAKE (9) appears on the right and that of WELLINGTON (10) 100 feet high, stands out on the left.

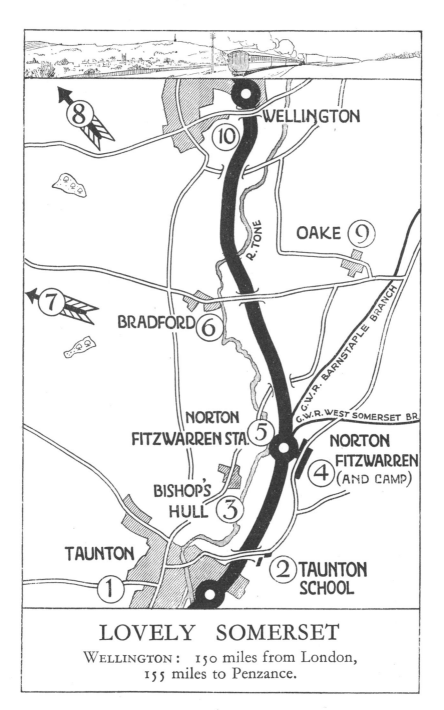

LOVELY SOMERSET

WELLINGTON: 150 miles from London,
155 miles to Penzance.

WELLINGTON TO BURLESCOMBE

Wellington

THERE are two Wellingtons—one in Somerset and one in Shropshire. The Somerset WELLINGTON (1) is the one from which the great Iron Duke took his title, although he was not of local descent. He was lord of the ancient manor of Wellington, the records of which are traced right back to the time when it was held by Asser, Bishop of Sherborne, and preceptor to Alfred the Great. The fine red sandstone tower of Wellington Church rises prominently above the town, which is a busy little market centre, with woollen factories and paper mills.

The steepled church noticed on the left just after clearing Wellington itself is that of the suburb of ROCKWELL GREEN (2). Away across country on the same side is the WELLINGTON MONU-MENT (3) which has been a prominent landmark ahead for the last few miles of the journey. It stands 900 feet above sea-level on a summit of the BLACKDOWN HILLS (4), from which fine banks of trees run down into the valley. The monument is in the form of an obelisk 160 feet high erected in honour of the victor of Waterloo.

Sampford Arundel

The church tower which is presently passed on the left side of the line is that of SAMPFORD ARUNDEL (5), and behind it at a distance of about two miles CULMSTOCK BEACON (6) rises to a height of 600 feet at the western end of the Blackdown range. From this spur the country slopes away into the CULM VALLEY (7).

The approach to WHITEBALL TUNNEL (8) is up a fairly stiff gradient, and some hard snorting is heard as the powerful engine pounds its way up the rise. The tunnel is about two-thirds of a mile long, and somewhere in its dark recesses we cross the frontier from smiling Somerset into glorious Devon. The big main road from Taunton to the West, which has been keeping us company on the right for some distance takes advantage of the tunnel to slip over our heads and now travels across country to the left on its way to Tiverton. Across to the right are the great stone quarries of Whiteball and the church of HOLCOMBE ROGUS (9). The second part of the name is not bogus by any means,

Burlescombe Quarries

since it is derived from that of Rogo who held this place in Norman times.

On the left is presently seen the tower of BURLESCOMBE CHURCH (10), and in another moment or two we are flying through BURLESCOMBE STATION (11), with the lie of the land now in our favour for speed-making.

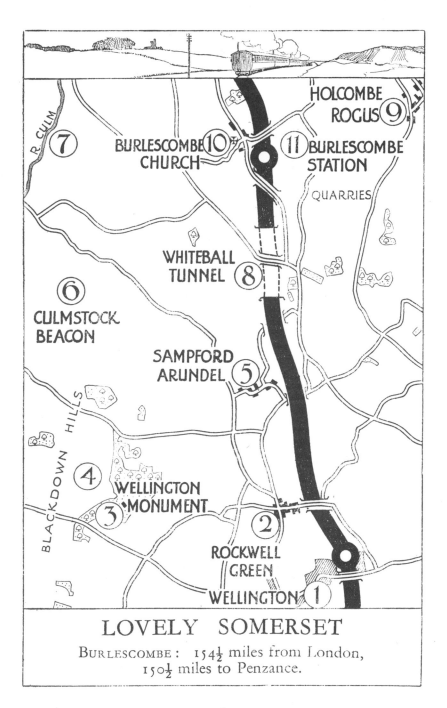

R. CULM

⑦

HOLCOMBE ROGUS ⑨

BURLESCOMBE CHURCH ⑩

⑪ BURLESCOMBE STATION

QUARRIES

WHITEBALL TUNNEL ⑧

⑥ CULMSTOCK BEACON

SAMPFORD ARUNDEL ⑤

BLACKDOWN HILLS

④

WELLINGTON MONUMENT ③

②

ROCKWELL GREEN

WELLINGTON ①

LOVELY SOMERSET

Burlescombe: $154\frac{1}{2}$ miles from London, $150\frac{1}{2}$ miles to Penzance.

DARTMOOR.

GLORIOUS DEVON

Exeter.   E. Margaret Holman.

GLORIOUS DEVON

THE broad county of Devon, glorious alike in song and in history as the home of the great sea-rovers of Elizabeth's time, not only brings together several sharply defined types of landscape, but succeeds in welding them into a coherent whole by some strange power that seems to amount almost to conscious art. Although Dartmoor has such a strong individuality of its own in the rugged grandeur of its rocky tors standing out in silhouette on the sky-line, and in its vast expanse of solitary country over which you may tramp for miles without meeting a soul or hearing a sound except the cry of a bird, it joins up without any awkwardness or abrupt division to that other type of Devon's inland scenery—the warm and inviting wooded valleys in which old villages nestle and where the smoke from quaint old cottages makes a blue cloud among the trees.

And these two types both merge again with a fine harmony into that glorious coastline which is the chief pride of Devon, with its towering cliffs and golden sands, sheltered combes and curving bays. In the course of our long run of eighty miles or so through Devon we shall see all of these things in rich variety, crossing almost innumerable rivers which have in many cases well-wooded banks, running alongside the sea with the waves almost lapping the permanent way on one side while cliffs tower up on the other, and gaining many a peep at distant masses of jagged rocks which mark the summits of Dartmoor.

That is Devonshire treated on broad lines. But when we come down from the general to the particular, what a wonderful succession of intensely interesting towns and villages and picturesque " sights " of other kinds are seen in passing glimpse on this stage of our journey—Exeter, with its cathedral, the broad sands and shipping of the Exe estuary, Teignmouth's quaint old bridge straddling the mouth of the Teign, the wooded country around Newton Abbot, the great beacons at the southern edge of Dartmoor, the ancient castle of Totnes, prehistoric camps and burial mounds, and—as the culminating point of interest where the Cornish Riviera Express makes its first stop—Plymouth, with its maze of naval craft and mercantile shipping, its memories of Drake and the Pilgrim Fathers. These are but a few points gathered haphazard from the rich store of picturesque Devon.

Nor is it possible to see these things without feeling something of the fine spirit of adventure which is the proud inheritance of all Devonians. The marks and symbols of it appear both inland and on the coast—here a house which was the home of the Raleighs, there the Hoe upon which Drake played his game of bowls, the curious Warren at Dawlish which was once a smugglers' haunt, and scores of ancient castles with many a tale of siege and sally.

Devon is assuredly a county with a personality.

BURLESCOMBE TO CULLOMPTON

Burlescombe

THE disused canal which is close to the railway on the right a little way beyond Burlescombe Station is the GRAND WESTERN CANAL **(1)**. This connects the River Tone—from which Taunton derives its name—with the Exe, which the canal enters at Tiverton. It runs alongside us for a short distance and then suddenly turns off to the right and goes across country to SAMPFORD PEVEREL **(2)**, which we can easily locate by the tower of its church. Quarries of a wonderful pink stone appear on the same side of the line, cut into the hillsides which slope upwards to the north to culminate in the wild expanse of EXMOOR **(3)**.

Travelling down almost due south between the hills, through a pleasant pastoral landscape dotted with many an old farmhouse and a great gathering place of small streams which will go eventually to swell the waters of the Exe, we pass through TIVERTON JUNCTION **(4)**. Here a branch line turns off to serve the pleasant old town of Tiverton, which lies tucked away in the valley of the Exe about five miles almost due west from the junction. It is a great sportsman's centre, where a man may take his choice of stag, fox, hare or otter hunting, or devote himself to excellent fishing. Tiverton has a magnificent church.

Sampford Peverel

To the north-west—still looking to the right of the line—BARTON HILL **(5)** reaches a height of 787 feet about three miles distant from Tiverton, marking a stretch of country in which frequent patches of woodland appear as surviving relics of the great Exmoor Forest.

Over to the left, looking across the CULM VALLEY **(6)** the village church of KENTISBEARE **(7)** is seen rising above its surrounding trees. The Culm River is an important tributary of the Exe, coming down from the southern slopes of the Blackdown Hills and gathering the waters of many smaller rivulets in the vale through which we are travelling. One of these is the SPRATFORD STREAM **(8)** which winds pleasantly through the country to the right of us, passing under the Tiverton branch line a little way from the junction and afterwards flowing close beside the main line.

Cullompton

CULLOMPTON **(9)**, which we are now approaching, is a quiet, quaint little place nowadays, but once had a busy woollen manufacture. It shows a fine church tower of reddish stone, which, judging from the colour, must surely have come from one of the quarries we have lately passed.

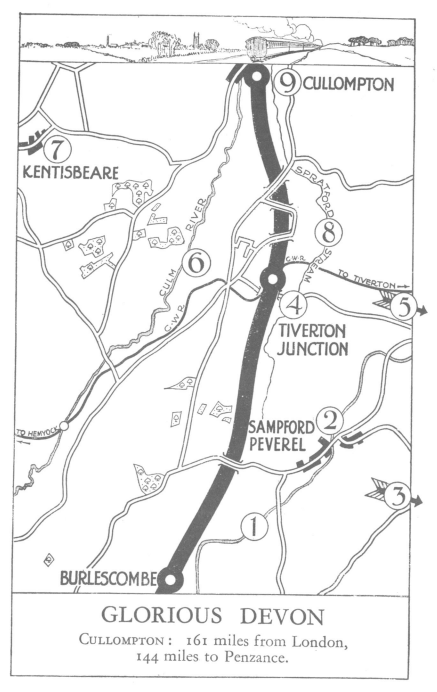

GLORIOUS DEVON

CULLOMPTON: 161 miles from London,
144 miles to Penzance.

CULLOMPTON TO SILVERTON

River Culm

A mile south from **Cullompton Station** the railway crosses the **River Culm (1)** which now takes a winding course close beside the line on the right. The Taunton to Exeter main road, after passing through Cullompton, crosses over on to our left, comes up to the line-side opposite Bradninch and then swerves off again and disappears behind the great bulk of Dolbury Hill.

On the gradually rising ground to the right now appears the village of Bradninch (2), one of the most interesting old places in Devon. It now displays a big new factory in abrupt contrast to the purely agricultural character of the surrounding countryside. Bradninch was a chartered borough as long ago as 1208, and from the time of Edward II. to that of Henry VII. returned two Members of Parliament. But the good citizens of Bradninch found Parliamentary representation more of a nuisance than a privilege, and what is more had the moral courage to say so, with the result that Henry VII. excused them on payment of a fine of five marks, equivalent to £3 16s. 3d.

Bradninch Manor House, which stands to the right on the outskirts of the village, furnishes one of the finest specimens of a rich Elizabethan interior in the country. Some of the rooms are splendidly panelled and carved. Charles I. stayed at the old Rectory during the Civil War.

Hele Paper Mill

Hele and Bradninch Station (3) is about a mile from Bradninch village, but quite close to the smaller hamlet of Hele (4), where a paper factory is set close beside the Culm. The river passes under the railway again soon afterwards.

The wooded hill which shows up prominently close to the railway on the left, rising up from Kileston Park, is known as Dolbury Hill (5) upon which are the entrenchments of a pre-historic camp. The hill is well wooded on the railway side. Rising sharply out of the landscape, it checks the River Culm on its course and forces it to make a wide semi-circular detour on which it comes right up to the railway again. The mystery which hovers over Dolbury Hill because of the traces of pre-historic man

Dolbury Hill

graven upon it is increased when we hear of the legend which declares that a great treasure lies buried within it.

Beneath the shadow of Dolbury Hill is Silverton Station (6), and a little more than a mile across country to the right is Silverton (7) itself, set where the hills subside into the vale.

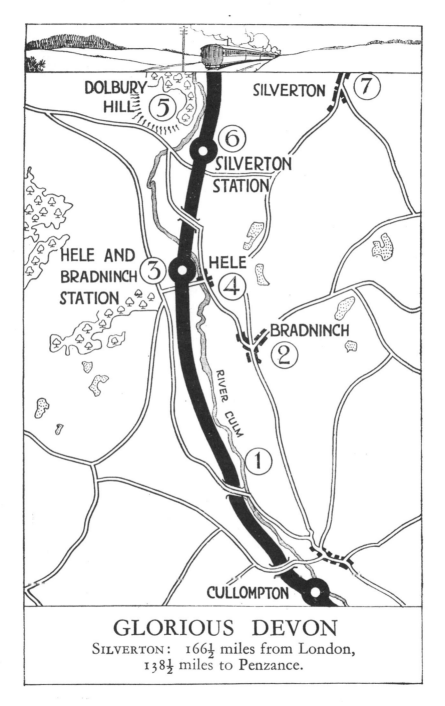

DOLBURY HILL ⑤

SILVERTON ⑦

⑥ SILVERTON STATION

HELE AND BRADNINCH STATION ③

HELE ④

BRADNINCH ②

RIVER CULM

①

CULLOMPTON

GLORIOUS DEVON

SILVERTON: $166\frac{1}{2}$ miles from London,
$138\frac{1}{2}$ miles to Penzance.

SILVERTON TO EXETER

Rewe Church

THE triangular stretch of lowland in which the Culm and the Exe join forces is closely surrounded by points of varied interest. The CULM (1) is on our left, and the winding EXE (2) is now seen drawing rapidly nearer to the right.

On the map the Culm presents the idea of a tangled skein of worsted in its final contortions before making complete surrender of its identity. It divides into two streams, one of which comes close up to the railway at REWE (3), the church tower of which is seen at close range on the left. But the two streams have become united again before reaching STOKE CANON (4), which gives us another church tower a mile beyond Rewe.

By this time the Exe has come to within half a mile of us on the right, and immediately across this picturesquely winding river now appears the church of BRAMPFORD SPEKE (5), rebuilt in 1853. Speke was the name of an ancient family which formerly held the lordship of the manor. Their coats-of-arms, with those of other notable families connected with this ancient parish, make a brave show in the windows of the church.

Stoke Woods

Beyond STOKE CANON STATION (6) the Exe passes under the railway to receive the waters of the Culm a quarter of a mile away to the left, with the beautiful STOKE WOODS (7) banking up finely on the lower slopes of the hills which run down to the river.

The Exe is a beautiful and interesting river, beginning its story away up amid the hills and woods and rocky tors of Exmoor. With that strange perversity characteristic of rivers, it rises at the centre of Exmoor Forest only five miles from the North Devon coast, but deliberately sets out on a wandering journey through the third largest English county until it finds its way into the sea on the South Devon coast at Exmouth. At Tiverton it receives the River Lowman, made famous by Blackmore in " Lorna Doone." It is closely hemmed in by rising ground until it reaches the point at which we have just made its acquaintance, and here the landscape spreads itself out in more level fashion, giving the river the chance to wind more than ever out of the pure luxury of laziness instead of

Exeter

by sheer stress of geographical circumstances. The Exe, by the way, is a fine river for fishermen.

Now the ancient city of EXETER (8) spreads itself out upon its hill to the left and we must look out for its famous cathedral. EXETER ST. DAVID'S STATION (9) marks our entry to the city.

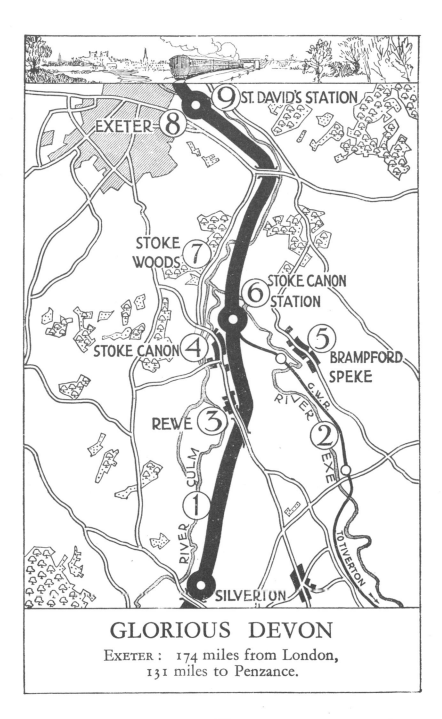

GLORIOUS DEVON

EXETER : 174 miles from London,
131 miles to Penzance.

EXETER TO EXMINSTER

Canal below Exeter

CURIOUSLY enough, the cathedral is one of the last things one sees on the passing glimpse of EXETER (1) which this journey affords. It has no sky-scraper of a tower like Gloucester ; it is inclined to be long, low and squat, and a great mass of other buildings range themselves in front of it and claim attention until somewhere about EXETER ST. THOMAS STATION (2) we have come sufficiently round the hill to obtain a fair broadside view of the famous and beautiful minster, with its twin towers standing not at the west end in the common Gothic convention, but striking a fresh note by occupying the position of transepts.

Exeter is one of the oldest cities of the West Country and has always been a capital in a much wider sense than that of being the county town of Devon, although that is a high distinction. In English history and art and government and all the things that go to make up a national culture, its position here in the West is very much like that of Winchester to the ancient kingdom of Wessex. In Exeter ancient buildings of all kinds—civil as well as religious—rub shoulders with each other and preserve rich treasures of art and history. But that is only one side of the story. Exeter is also a busy commercial city with a population of more than 60,000, and it is a great railway centre.

Topsham

Leaving Exeter, we have the RIVER EXE (3) on our left, but the waterway nearest to the railway is the EXETER CANAL (4) which deals with the navigation problem presented by the broad and treacherous sandbanks of the Exe estuary in somewhat similar fashion to the canal which runs alongside the Severn up to Gloucester. This canal runs between the railway and the Exe for about five miles. It was one of the first canals constructed in England, having been commenced in Queen Elizabeth's time. The picturesque glimpses of shipping standing high above the level of the river show that we are now rapidly nearing the coast.

A mile and a half from Exeter the pinnacled tower of ALPHING-TON CHURCH (5) appears on the right, while to the left the ancient seaport of TOPSHAM (6) with its picturesque craft is seen

Exminster Church

across the Exe. It looks very Dutch—as though it were a picture painted by Jacob Maris. On the right is the village of EXMINSTER (7)—which would be a very good name for Exeter itself—showing a 15th century church containing one of the ornate Devonshire carved screens.

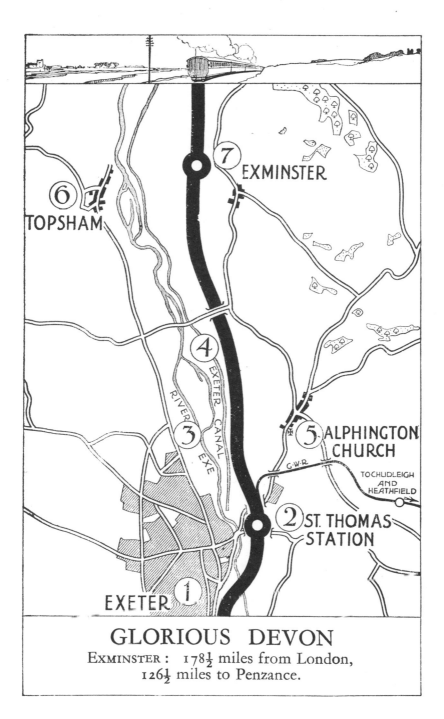

⑥ TOPSHAM

⑦ EXMINSTER

④

EXETER CANAL

RIVER EXE

③

⑤ ALPHINGTON CHURCH

G.W.R.

TO CHUDLEIGH AND HEATHFIELD

② ST. THOMAS STATION

EXETER ①

GLORIOUS DEVON

EXMINSTER: 178½ miles from London,
126½ miles to Penzance.

EXMINSTER TO DAWLISH WARREN

Powderham Castle

THE main road from Exeter to Dawlish and Teignmouth keeps us company on the right after passing through Exminster and then swerves farther inland to cut through the long strip of woodland which runs down to POWDERHAM (1), the ancient seat of the Earls of Devon.

High above the village rises BELVIDERE TOWER (2), or " Folly," set on a hill from which wide views are obtained over the estuary of the Exe. On the left NUTWELL COURT (2) is seen lying close beside the estuary. The great treasure of the house is a panel from Sir Francis Drake's ship, " The Golden Hind." The waterside village just beyond the mansion is LYMPSTONE (4).

Now the focus-point of interest shifts to the right again, for POWDERHAM CHURCH (5) shows up close at hand. In it beneath great monuments lie several generations of the great Courtenay family (Earls of Devon since 1533), who still hold their ancestral home of POWDERHAM CASTLE (6) which follows upon the church in quick succession, set in its spreading deer park. The castle was built about the time of the Norman Conquest and has been the home of the Courtenays since 1377.

Exmouth from Starcross

From STARCROSS (7), the station through which we pass about a mile beyond Powderham, there is a splendid view of EXMOUTH (8) across the great expanse of water. There is a good steamer service connecting Starcross station with this thriving and pretty seaside resort, which has a long sandy beach at the opening of the Exe into the sea. Between us and Exmouth as we travel south is that remarkable sandbank called DAWLISH WARREN (9) which thrusts itself out like a breakwater across the mouth of the river, and has golf links, bungalows and trees upon it. At the western end of it is DAWLISH WARREN STATION (10), with Langstone Cliff rising just beyond, at the point where the railway runs for the first time on this journey beside the open sea. A fine headland which rises on the opposite side of the estuary beyond Exmouth hides from view the seaside town of Budleigh Salterton, which lurks just round the corner.

Parson & Clerk

Fine cliffs of red sandstone rise on the landward side of us and we have a view, looking ahead from the left-hand side of the train, of the remarkable Parson and Clerk Rock. We shall soon pass within a few yards of it. DAWLISH (11) is the first seaside resort from London on the Cornish Riviera route.

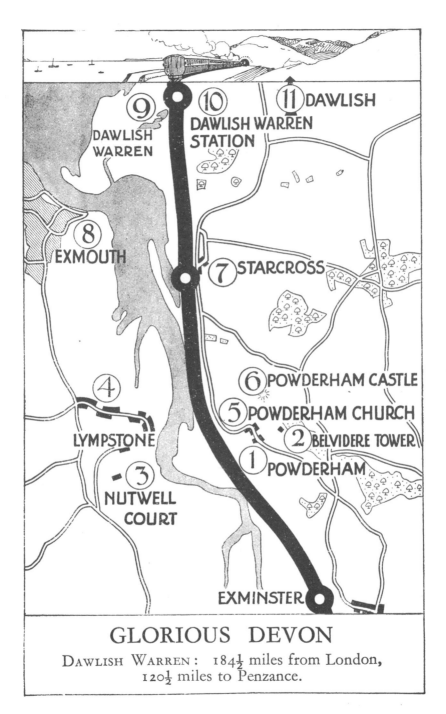

⑨ DAWLISH WARREN

⑧ EXMOUTH

⑩ DAWLISH WARREN STATION

⑪ DAWLISH

⑦ STARCROSS

④ LYMPSTONE

⑥ POWDERHAM CASTLE

⑤ POWDERHAM CHURCH

② BELVIDERE TOWER

① POWDERHAM

③ NUTWELL COURT

EXMINSTER

GLORIOUS DEVON

Dawlish Warren: $184\frac{1}{2}$ miles from London, $120\frac{1}{2}$ miles to Penzance.

DAWLISH WARREN TO TEIGNMOUTH

Dawlish

IN the old-time life of the South Devon coast, DAWLISH (1) figured as a favourite haunt of smugglers, who made use of the Warren we have lately seen and of various caves in the cliffs. Dawlish consists of two well-defined parts—an old town and a new town. The former, on the landward side, has the stream called the DAWLISH WATER (2) flowing through it and gains much picturesque charm thereby, while the coastal developments of the place appeal strongly to modern tastes with good hotels, shops and entertainments.

Travelling south from Dawlish, the line passes in quick succession through a number of short tunnels more or less reminiscent of the avalanche shelters on trans-Alpine routes. As we rush in and out of these burrows in the rock charming glimpses of the sea appear at one moment to be cut off abruptly at the next. First comes KENNAWAY TUNNEL (3), about 300 yards long, follwed by Phillot Tunnel (47 yards). Clerk's Tunnel obviously takes its name from one of the gentlemen depicted in that fine piece of Nature's sculpture which we have already seen from a distance and which now lies immediately ahead. Coryton Tunnel is namesake to CORYTON COVE (4), one of the minor indentations of the coast, and then comes PARSON'S TUNNEL (5), the last and longest of the series.

The Rail by the Sea

In travelling through this tunnel, which is rather more than a quarter of a mile long, we pass within a few yards of PARSON AND CLERK ROCK (6). Of course there is a story about Parson and Clerk Rock—that curious outpost of sandstone cliff worn by wind and weather into the quaint semblance of an old-time parson in his pulpit, with his clerk below—and it is told in the second volume of " Legendland," * which is a charming introduction to the myths and traditions of Devon and Cornwall. Looking back to see the strange profile in reverse, we may look also across the wide expanse of sea to where the Devon coast runs into Dorset to the east, giving on a fine day a glorious panorama of vari-coloured cliffs stretching right away to Portland Bill.

Teignmouth

Half a mile beyond Parson's Tunnel commence the outskirts of TEIGNMOUTH (7), a highly picturesque seaside resort, as well as a seaport in a small way of business, at the mouth of the RIVER TEIGN (8). The Danes raided it hundreds of years ago and the French in 1690.

* " Legendland " published by the G.W.R. Four Vols. 6d. each.

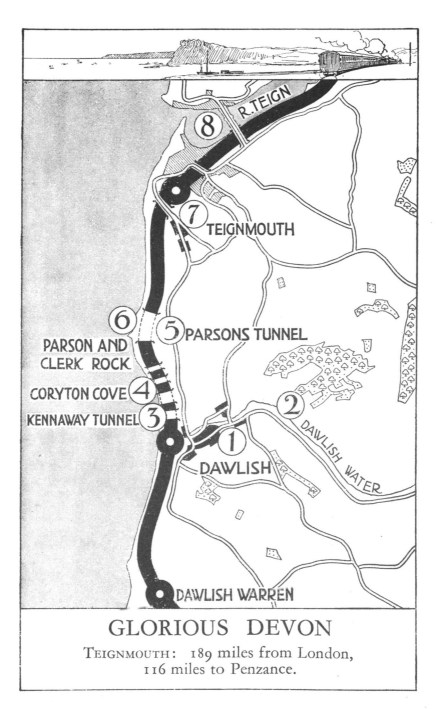

R.TEIGN

8

7 TEIGNMOUTH

6

5 PARSONS TUNNEL

PARSON AND
CLERK ROCK

CORYTON COVE 4

KENNAWAY TUNNEL 3

2

1

DAWLISH WATER

DAWLISH

DAWLISH WARREN

GLORIOUS DEVON

TEIGNMOUTH: 189 miles from London,
116 miles to Penzance.

TEIGNMOUTH TO NEWTON ABBOT

The Ness Rock

ACROSS the estuary the village of
SHALDON (1) lies at the waterside beneath
the shadow of NESS ROCK (2), a wooded
bluff which rises abruptly above the sea.
We feel that it really ought to have a
mediæval fortress frowning at us from
the top of it.

Now another highly-picturesque sub-
ject comes into the picture on the same side (the left) and that is
TEIGNMOUTH BRIDGE (3), the longest wooden bridge in England.
It was constructed in 1827, and carries the road from Teignmouth to Torquay across the estuary. The bridge is nearly a
third of a mile long. It has 34 arches and a drawbridge in the
middle to enable ships to pass through.

At Teignmouth the line turns inland alongside the Teign,
whose estuary spreads itself out over banks of sand. The village
of BISHOP'S TEIGNTON (4) seen on the right had an ancient importance through its close association with the Bishops of Exeter, who
had a country residence here. The ruins of the BISHOP'S PALACE
(5) built by Bishop Grandison in 1350 are upon the hillside above
the village at a spot called Radaway.
Only fragments of its walls now remain.

The LITTLE HALDON HILLS (6) which
stretch inland beyond the site of the
Bishop's Palace, are foot-hills to the vast
expanse of DARTMOOR (7) which forms
the wild and rugged hinterland of this
part of Devon. The most easily recog-

River Teign

nised characteristic of the Dartmoor landscape is, of course, its
numerous " tors " strewn with broken masses of rock, disposed
with such a fine irregularity as to suggest that the hill is a volcano
which has blown up at some time or other, and that the mighty
debris lies as it fell. One of the finest of these is seen from near
KING'S TEIGNTON (8), for across country to the right appears
rugged HAYTOR (9), 1,400 feet high, crowned by a spectacular
heap of rocks which, tradition says, were "enormous altars
into whose stone basins human blood flowed from hecatombs
of sacrificial victims." Ugh ! But tradition is probably very
wide of the mark. The writer from whom we have quoted
adds that "they were certainly never so used either by the
gentle-mannered aborigines or anyone
else."

At Newton Abbot

NEWTON ABBOT RACECOURSE (10) is
seen on the right, and a moment later we
tear through the important junction of
NEWTON ABBOT (11), a pleasant town at
the head of the Teign estuary and a good
centre for Dartmoor.

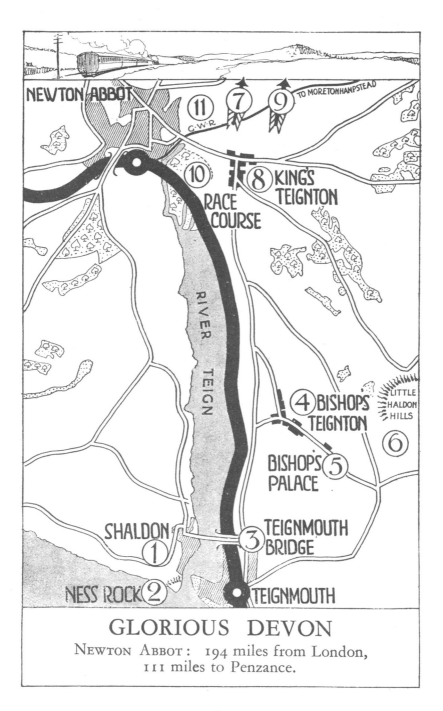

GLORIOUS DEVON

NEWTON ABBOT: 194 miles from London,
111 miles to Penzance.

NEWTON ABBOT TO TOTNES

St. Augustine's Priory

ABOUT a mile beyond Newton Abbot Station, the main line to TORQUAY (1) veers off to the left, the beautiful sub-tropical resort lying about five miles to the south.

On the right are seen the buildings of ST. AUGUSTINE'S PRIORY (2), a large modern convent of Canonesses Regular of the Lateran an order with a most interesting history. When the ancient Abbey of Burnham in Buckinghamshire, founded in 1265, was dissolved by Henry VIII., a nun crossed to Flanders and succeeded in establishing an English convent of the same Order in Louvain in 1609. In 1794 the French Revolution drove the nuns back to England and after living in succession at Hammersmith, Amesbury Abbey in Wiltshire, and at Spettisbury in Dorset, the community came to Newton Abbot in 1861. The convent, which has a magnificent church, thus forms an interesting link with pre-Reformation England.

The village seen beyond the Priory is ABBOTS KERSWELL (3) in the name of which there is an obvious harking-back to ancient monastic associations. The name distinguishes it from KINGSKERSWELL (4) which lies on our left, and has a station on the Torquay line. The picturesque church tower shows up as we pass.

Bourton Hall

The line climbs up between rugged cliffs and quarry workings in the red and pink stone of Dainton Hill until DAINTON TUNNEL (5) is reached at the summit. Then the view opens out again. Looking up the valley to the right, a long succession of views of DARTMOOR (6) is obtained, with distant tors showing their rocky crests in silhouette on the sky-line. On this side also appears the village of LITTLE HEMPSTON (7) identified by the lofty tower of its ancient church. The place is alternatively known as Hempston Arundel because the Arundel family held the manor for a long period.

On the left appears BOURTON HALL (8) a large house of prominent situation, which, especially when it catches the sun, stands out as a big white patch on the landscape. We are now descending into the Dart valley. The ASHBURTON BRANCH (9) now

Totnes

joins us on the right, and immediately afterwards the RIVER DART (10) is crossed. The church tower of TOTNES (11) already shows up ahead to the left and we pass through the picturesque old town, an admirable centre from which to explore Dartmoor and the lovely valley of the Dart.

84

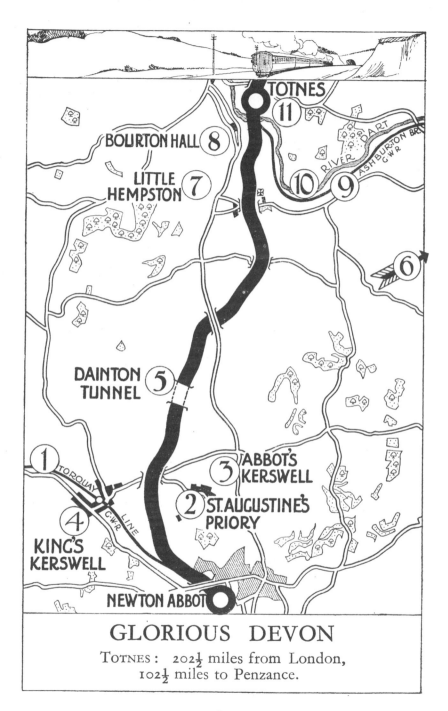

GLORIOUS DEVON

TOTNES: 202½ miles from London,
102½ miles to Penzance.

TOTNES TO BRENT

Totnes Castle

THE highest ground in Totnes is occupied by the ivy-covered keep of its fine old Norman CASTLE (1) which dominates the town and provides a splendid view-point for a wide stretch of landscape. The building of it is attributed to a Norman baron named Judhael who came to England with the Conqueror, but probably additions were made at later periods. The grounds, by the way, are open to the public.

A little farther along on the same side of the line (the left) FOLLATON HOUSE (2) stands close beside the railway in a park of 160 acres. The line now serpentines through the landscape with hills rising up on either side, the country on the right being part of the vast expanse of DARTMOOR (3). The modern church noticed close beside the line on that side is that of TIGLEY (4). A little farther inland on the same side the church steeple of RATTERY (5) is seen. The church is one of those which help to make Devon famous for its carved oak screens. About four miles across country in the same direction lies Buckfastleigh, where Benedictine monks have in recent years built a new Abbey to take the place of the one destroyed at the Reformation, of which a few fragments remain.

Follaton House

The stream alongside the railway on the left is the HARBORNE RIVER (6) which rises about three miles across country to the right, and, flowing under the railway just beyond Rattery, winds through the hills to escape into the Dart just before that river enters the sea. After crossing the Harborne we plunge into MARLEY TUNNEL (7), half a mile long and on emerging have a good view of BRENT HILL (8) which rises to a height of 1,017 feet ahead of us to the right. On the top of it are the ruins of an ancient chapel dedicated to St. Michael. Broad views are gained from its summit, including vast stretches of Dartmoor, the Teign Valley and glimpses of the open sea.

At the foot of Brent Hill on its western side flows the Devonshire AVON (9)—one of many rivers bearing that name—and where the river flows beneath the railway stands the village of BRENT (10), which is more strictly to be called South Brent. The hilly country stretching northwards from here on either side of the Avon—or "the Aune," as it is locally called—is thickly strewn with pre-historic hut circles and other vestiges of remote occupation, while about four miles above Brent the ancient track known as the Abbot's Way fords the river.

Brent Hill

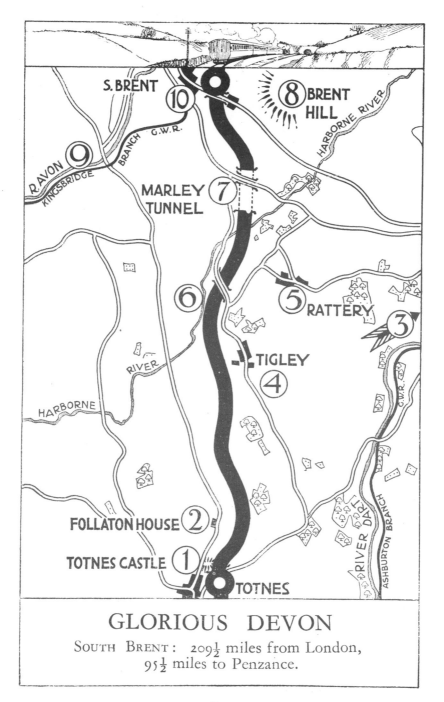

GLORIOUS DEVON

South Brent: 209½ miles from London,
95½ miles to Penzance.

BRENT TO IVYBRIDGE

Western Beacon

THE rushing stream of the Avon which we cross at Brent Station gives a delightful sense of coolness on a hot summer's day. Beyond Brent some of the prominent heights of the southern fringe of the Dartmoor country occupy the picture ahead. Chief among these is UGBOROUGH BEACON (1), seen first of all from the left-hand side of the train at Brent and then on the right as the railway curves round to the south. At the crossing of the little GLAZE BROOK (2) about a mile beyond Brent we have a peep up the valley to the long ridge of UGBOROUGH MOOR (3) of which the Beacon is the culminating point. On the Moor are many stone circles, hut circles, tumuli and other relics of a vanished race. The village of UGBOROUGH (4) lies a mile from the railway to the left, hidden from sight by an intervening hill.

After passing through WRANGATON STATION (5) and BITTAFORD PLATFORM (6), where the large buildings of Plymouth Asylum are seen near to the station, the railway comes alongside Ugborough Beacon's next-door neighbour, WESTERN BEACON (7), which rises to 1,130 feet, just a hundred feet short of Ugborough Beacon. At this point we have a preliminary peep at an industry which is really more characteristic of Cornwall, for large CHINA CLAY WORKS (8) are set close beside the line at the foot of Western Beacon.

Ugborough Moor

The spired church of IVYBRIDGE (9) now shows up ahead and in another mile the village is reached, with STOWFORD HOUSE (10) showing up on the right just before we cross the wooded valley of the RIVER ERME (11). Ivybridge takes its name from a bridge across the Erme here possessing the proud distinction of being in no less than four parishes, each of which claims one part of it. No doubt the discussions as to who should mend such a bridge in pre-County Council days would have provided all the raw material for the libretto of a Gilbert and Sullivan comic opera. The bridge was formerly covered with ivy, but whether the name resulted from this or whether the ivy was deliberately planted and tended in order to help the place to live up to its name is a fine point for research.

Ivybridge

The most beautiful part of the Erme Valley is precisely the part of which we now have a passing glimpse, extending north between wooded banks from Ivybridge to HARFORD (12), a favourite pleasure resort in the summer on account of the fine river and moorland scenery at Tor Rocks and Neaford.

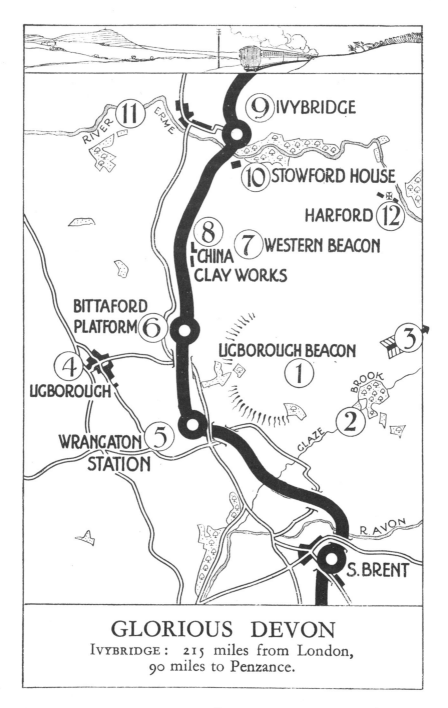

GLORIOUS DEVON

IVYBRIDGE : 215 miles from London,
90 miles to Penzance.

IVYBRIDGE TO PLYMPTON

Fardell House

A fine expanse of landscape with frequent patches of woodland opens out to the left as we travel out of the Erme Valley at Ivybridge towards the Yealm Valley which runs parallel with it a few miles farther west. On the right, the Dartmoor side, HENLAKE DOWN (1) and HANGAR DOWN (2) rise close together, the former 696 feet and the latter 753 feet high.

FARDELL (3) to the left of the line was formerly the seat of the Raleigh family from which came the great Sir Walter, although their real home-place was Hayes Barton Manor, near Sidmouth. Some remains of the mansion in which Sir Walter's father lived at Fardell still exist and show among other details the ancient private chapel.

The railway now crosses the RIVER YEALM (4) the collector of the waters of half a dozen moorland streams a couple of miles up country to the right and comes down through CORNWOOD (5) and alongside the charming patch of woodland amid which is CORNWOOD STATION (6). At the other end of the wood the PIALL RIVER (7) flows under the line to join the Yealm about half a mile down the wooded valley to the left.

Beechwood Park

Splendid views open up on the right looking north to PENN MOOR (8) and LEE MOOR (9), which are dotted with pre-historic burial mounds, remains of stone circles, and, on the west side of Penn Moor, those of a chambered hut.

PENN BEACON (10) rises 1,407 feet high. This countryside is a fascinating area for exploration not merely on archæological grounds, but because innumerable streams plunge recklessly down the hillsides with frequent cascades and waterfalls. The scenery is not on the grand scale, perhaps, but it is very lovely.

On the right soon after crossing Piall River is BEECHWOOD PARK (11), the residence of Lord Seaton, and a mile farther along on the same side is HEMERDON HOUSE (12). Just behind it to the north rises HEMERDON BALL (13), a tree-crowned hill 700 feet high where a big camp was established at the time of the Napoleonic wars. The village to the left of the railway is RIDGEWAY (14)

Hemerdon Ball

Now we cross TORY BROOK (15) which comes down from Penn Moor and pass through PLYMPTON (16) an ancient town now almost submerged in the suburban developments of Plymouth. Plympton's chief claim to distinction lies in the fact that Sir Joshua Reynolds was born here in 1723.

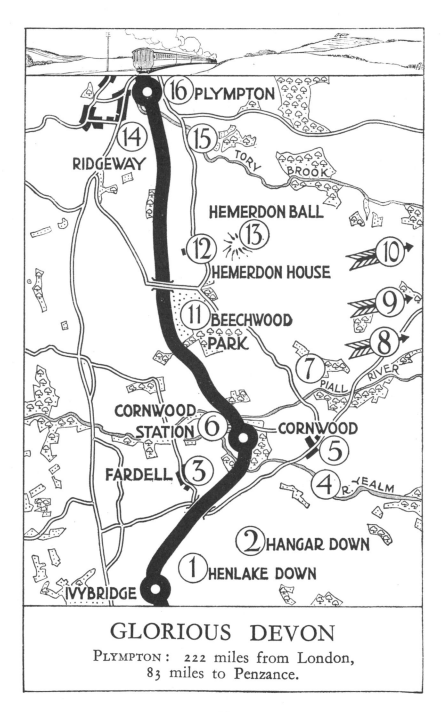

GLORIOUS DEVON

PLYMPTON : 222 miles from London,
83 miles to Penzance.

PLYMPTON TO PLYMOUTH

Efford Fort

THE fine tower seen to the left in passing through PLYMPTON (1) is that of the parish church of St. Mary, at one time the mother church of Plymouth. There is something fantastic in the idea of Plympton being the mother of Plymouth, but English topography is full of such curiosities. Both towns obviously derive their names from their situations on the RIVER PLYM (2) which is tidal at the point where we now cross it. On the right is seen EFFORD FORT (3), one of the old fortifications of Plymouth, built well into the hillside.

The Plym now flows close alongside on the left, and looking down stream the great port of PLYMOUTH (4) is seen, the tangled forest of shipping mingling in semi-obscurity with the smoke from factories and houses. The hard outlines of fortifications mark the high ground above PLYMOUTH SOUND (5).

We have shut off steam now and the engine driver is " feeling " the train with his brakes as we slide down into Plymouth town through a little string of suburban stations—LAIRA HALT (6) at the outskirts, Lipson Vale Halt, then the short run through MUTLEY TUNNEL (7) and through MUTLEY STATION (8), and then—wonder of wonders !—we actually stop, for here is PLYMOUTH NORTH ROAD (9), 225¾ miles from Paddington.

River coming down to Plymouth

Plymouth, of course, is a fascinating place, with the history of England and the Empire written all over it in plain figures. Here you may tread the identical HOE (10) on which Drake finished his game of bowls in the true English spirit before turning to fight the Armada. Here, too, is the veritable strip of quay from which the Pilgrim Fathers stepped aboard the " Mayflower." And yet those events were on a small scale compared with the gigantic part played by Plymouth and her twin-sister DEVONPORT (11) in the Great War—not only on the naval side, though that was supreme —but with the swollen ranks of her garrison and the tense activity of the airmen who flew from the base on the CATTEWATER (12).

In passing through Plymouth we have many glimpses of its busy streets, always with a good sprinkling of naval uniform, and run

The Hamoaze & Dockyard

along the ends of innumerable back gardens, every one of which has a mast with pulleys and ropes to manipulate the domestic clothes-line in the strict naval tradition. Plymouth marks an important stage of the journey for here we take farewell of Devon and a few minutes after re-starting enter Cornwall.

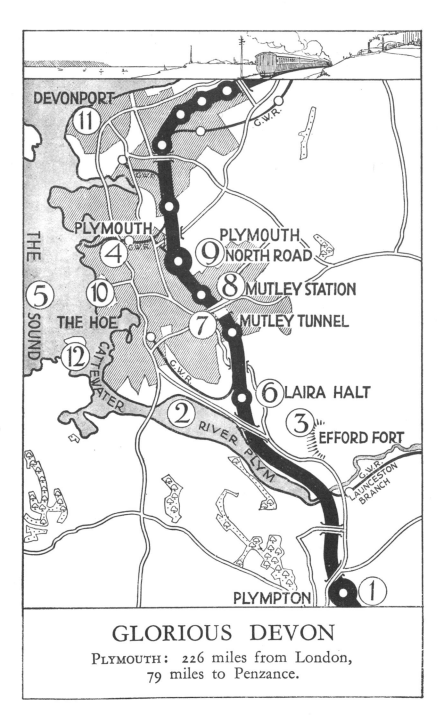

GLORIOUS DEVON

PLYMOUTH: 226 miles from London,
79 miles to Penzance.

PLYMOUTH TO SALTASH

The great naval base of DEVONPORT (1) joins Plymouth on the west, and the famous Dockyards of the Royal Navy stretch for a couple of miles along the HAMOAZE (2), which is the broad estuary through which the rivers Tamar, Tavy and Lynher find their way into Plymouth Sound. The land seen across the Hamoaze, round about the village of TORPOINT (3), is our first sight of Cornwall. It forms a peninsular between the LYNHER or ST. GERMAN'S RIVER (4) and the sea

As we leave Devonport interest is chiefly centred in the crowded shipping of the Hamoaze, in which naval craft of many types and sizes are predominant, and in the immense bridge now seen ahead from the left of the train. This is the great ROYAL ALBERT BRIDGE (5) at Saltash, which crosses the RIVER TAMAR (6) just before the latter joins the St. German's River to form the Hamoaze. The train approaches it through another string of local stations —and across Weston Mill Lake to ST. BUDEAUX (7).

The Royal Albert Bridge at Saltash, built for the sole purpose of carrying the Great Western Railway across the river, was named in honour of Queen Victoria's husband, the Prince Consort. It is one of the best-known achievements of I. K. Brunel, who constructed the Great Western Railway, and ranks with the Forth and Tay bridges as a daring and spectacular piece of engineering. We have already had a good broadside view of it from Devonport. To look up at it from a small boat on the Hamoaze or the Tamar is to gain an impression of something too mighty to be real—a vast piece of imagination. It was, of course, even more of a marvel when it was first opened in 1859 than it is now. The two main spans are each of 445 feet, and there are seventeen smaller spans of about 69 feet each, the total length of the bridge being 2,240 feet—nearly half a mile.

We cross the Hamoaze at a height of 100 feet above high water level, gaining magnificent views of the estuary with its shipping to the left and up the Tamar Valley to the right. At the far end of the bridge is SALTASH (8), and we have arrived in CORNWALL

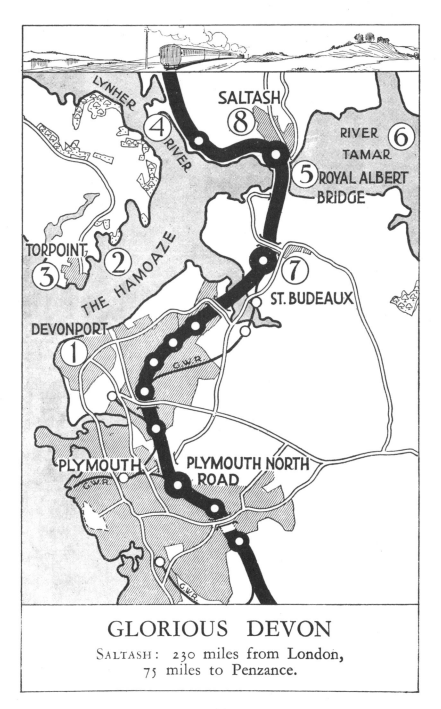

GLORIOUS DEVON

SALTASH: 230 miles from London,
75 miles to Penzance.

SALTASH BRIDGE.

THE
CORNISH
RIVIERA

St. Michael's Mount.

THE CORNISH RIVIERA

AND now for the "delectable Duchy," the English Riviera! These are high-sounding names. Can it be that any part of England succeeds in living up to them? We shall see.

To speak of Cornwall as "the Duchy" is to remember that one of the ancient titles held by the Royal House is that of Duke of Cornwall. But such a name as the English Riviera is a description and a challenge.

It has been suggested elsewhere in this book that Cornwall is so distinct from the rest of England as to seem almost another country. This holds true even if one judges only by such superficial characteristics as the names of railway stations and things seen from the carriage windows. Its truth is emphasized as one probes into history, legend and folk-lore, into the dead Cornish language and stories of the Cornish saints. Here, indeed, is a part of Britain with a culture and character peculiarly its own.

Even those least inclined for research cannot journey through Cornwall unconscious of its remoteness from the things that are ordinary and average. It is undeniably different from any other part of England through which the long journey has carried us. Names of stations beyond Plymouth tell something of the story— St. Budeaux, St. Blazey, St. Austell, St. Erth, St. Ives. We are in the land of Saints. A land where the Faith is very old.

But we have not come primarily on pilgrimage to the Land of Saints, although the tiny, picturesque churches dedicated to them, no less than the crumbling ruins and romantic caverns of the Arthurian legends, are among the things to see in Cornwall. The real charm of the Duchy and the justification of its claim to be considered the English Riviera is a matter of landscape and climate. Seascape would perhaps be a better term, since the grand scenery of Cornwall lies along her coasts, north and south. Seascapes framed in rugged rocks make up her panorama. One sees them at intervals as the train nears the sea at many points on its journey through the whole length of Cornwall. Now the north coast, now the south breaks into view, and when at last St. Michael's Mount rears its astonishing shape out of the sea, the picture seems too good to be true.

To appreciate the climate of Cornwall is not merely a matter of believing what the weather experts say. Palms growing on stations between Plymouth and Penzance remind us that here we are at Britain's farthest south, in a warm and genial climate that encourages luxurious growth of unfamiliar plants and flowers, but where the warmth is tempered always by fresh breezes from the sea.

Whichever way the wind blows in Cornwall it is a sea-breeze.

SALTASH TO ST. GERMANS

Trematon Castle

THE ivy-covered tower which now appears on the right is that of TREMATON CASTLE (1), which dates in part from the 13th century. The most interesting thing about it is that Sir Richard Grenville was once its governor, and with the naval traditions of Plymouth still fresh in our minds we are in the mood to recall the opening lines of a familiar poem of school days— "At Flores in the Azores, Sir Richard Grenville lay"—and to be thrilled afresh with the gallant story of the "Revenge."

To the left, across the broad estuary of the St. Germans or Lynher River, which flows into the Hamoaze just below Saltash, ANTONY HOUSE (2) is seen, set in a spreading park. This ancient seat of the Carews is happily still in the family, its present owner being Sir Reginald Pole-Carew. The Richard Carew who wrote a "Survey of Cornwall" in Elizabeth's time is buried in ANTONY CHURCH (3), a 15th century building, the embattled tower of which rises from the village which lies about a mile to the west of the Park. Evidently St. Anthony was a popular saint of mediæval Cornwall, as indeed of England generally, for this is one of three villages named after him in the Duchy.

Landmark on hill

Now we dive into SHILLINGHAM TUNNEL (4) for a quarter of a mile, and on emerging may look across country to the right, where the rounded summit of KIT HILL (5) rises to a height of 1,091 feet. It is easily identified by the tall mine chimney which rises from it. We shall become very familiar with these chimneys, mostly marking disused lead mines, as we journey through Cornwall.

On the opposite side of the line is another kind of LANDMARK (6) set on a hill-top commanding fine views across land and sea. This is a relic of the Great War, for it was erected at that period as a guide to airmen. The neighbouring coast and the expanse of sea beyond were the scene of great activity on the part of the Royal Naval Air Service, from its base on the Cattewater at Plymouth.

At a point due south from Kit Hill, the railway crosses the RIVER LYNHER (7), and in another mile the RIVER TIDDY (8) is crossed, sweeping round a fine curve at the foot of woodlands

River Tiddy

just before passing under the railway. Immediately beyond here we enter ST. GERMANS (9), a small town which was an ancient borough up to the time of the Reform Act. Its fine Norman Church is not visible from the railway, but the tower of ST. ERNY CHURCH (10), is seen across country to the right.

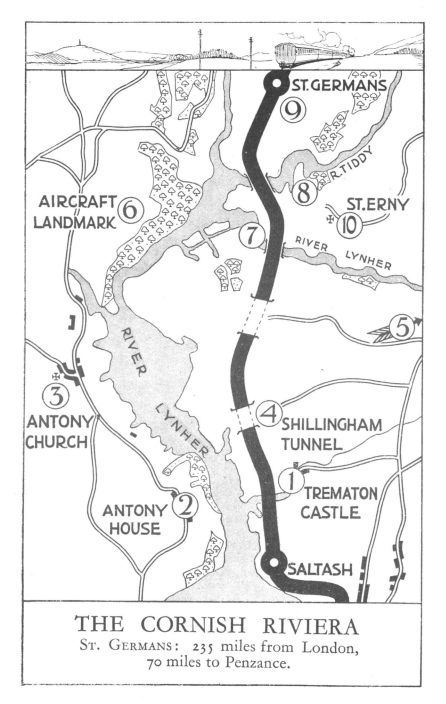

THE CORNISH RIVIERA

St. Germans: 235 miles from London,
70 miles to Penzance.

99

ST. GERMANS TO MENHENIOT

Kit Hill

IN passing through St. Germans, the trees of PORT ELIOT PARK (1), the seat of the Earl of St. Germans, will be seen on the right, and when the train is clear of the town KIT HILL (2) shows up again from a fresh angle. A little beyond and to the west of it is seen the tower of LANDRAKE CHURCH (3), while in the far distance, looking right across the Devonshire border to the north, is a fine view of DARTMOOR (4), whose rocky tors have been showing up at intervals over a long stretch of our journey.

And now, looking ahead again, the steeple of MENHENIOT CHURCH (5), where the famous William of Wykeham was once Rector, appears on the right only about a mile from the railway, while the high country seen in the same direction forms the outskirts of BODMIN MOOR (6) which shows up in irregular outline round about the Cheesewring, a mysterious cairn of prehistoric origin set on a hillside.

We are now in a land of hills separated by winding, zig-zagging valleys which the train crosses in quick succession by frequent viaducts. There are picturesque peeps of old stone-built Cornish cottages set down there beside the little streams that flow through the troughs of the valleys and turn many a water mill on their courses. The domestic architecture of Cornwall looks a trifle cold, perhaps, when one compares it mentally with timber and thatch or red-tiled roofs, but it is entirely in character with the landscape, which is inclined to be stern and often bleak in contrast to the more kindly Devonshire country. But bear in mind, please, that this is *not* the Cornish Riviera, but the fringe of the vast Bodmin Moor.

Menheniot Church

The train crosses the RIVER SEATON (7) which comes down from the moorland country to the north, and flows here between well-wooded banks, just before passing through MENHENIOT STATION (8).

CLICKER TOR (9) is a small hill to the left of the line which gains prominence out of all proportion to its height, only 468 feet, by the finely jagged silhouette of rocks strewn along the crest of it. The Tor rises close beside the railway and as the line curves round we see it from distinct points of view. The place is interesting to botanists because a rare kind of heath called *Erica Vagans* formerly grew here. The hill suggests a scrap of Dartmoor which has somehow got out of its bearings.

Clicker Tor

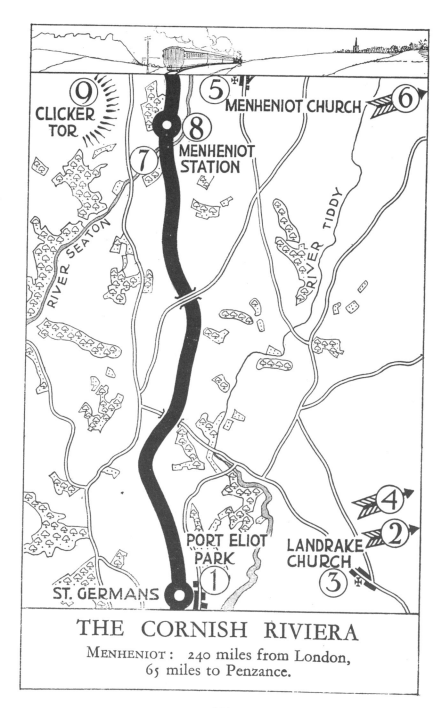

THE CORNISH RIVIERA

MENHENIOT: 240 miles from London,
65 miles to Penzance.

MENHENIOT TO LISKEARD

Liskeard Church

A mile and a half beyond ⁱMenheniot Station, the line crosses the MAIN ROAD **(1)**, which, starting from Torpoint facing Devonport across the Hamoaze, has been running more or less parallel with the railway for several miles on its way to LISKEARD **(2)**, one of the chief centres of life in West Cornwall. It is the tower of Liskeard Church, recently re-built, that now shows up ahead on the right hand side of the railway, a landmark set upon a hill. The church is the second largest in Cornwall.

Liskeard is a typical Cornish town set at the edge of the breezy uplands of Bodmin Moor, and is a splendid centre from which to explore a fascinating district. The CHEESEWRING **(3)** already mentioned, is a weird pile of rocks no less mysterious than Stonehenge. Speed marked them down on his map of Cornwall 300 years ago.

In the same romantic region are the mysterious DOGMARE POOL **(4)** set at the highest point of the moorlands; the TREVETHY STONE; the HURLERS, which are relics of prehistoric stone circles, and other unexplained monuments of prehistoric man, all with a wealth of tradition and quaint superstition attached to them. As "The 10.30 Limited" goes speeding through Liskeard we shall promise ourselves, if we are wise, a halt some day here for an excursion on to the great open spaces of Bodmin Moor, Cornwall's Salisbury Plain.

On the Moors

The road crossing the railway at Liskeard Station is one that has come up from the coast at Looe, keeping close to the River Looe all the way until it arrives within a mile and a half of Liskeard, its objective. Less than a mile beyond Liskeard Station the line crosses the LOOE RIVER **(5)** just above the village of Lamellion. The BRANCH LINE TO LOOE **(6)** turns off to the left here and, like the road, keeps close to the river on its way down to the sister-towns of East and West Looe, about seven miles distant to the south.

For the next few miles of the journey the right-hand side of the line offers the more interesting country, with fine views of BODMIN

Cornish Scenery

MOOR **(7)** opening up at intervals as the train crosses the valleys. This countryside has a certain "forlornness." Sir Arthur Quiller-Couch, speaks of the traveller being haunted by it as his road leads past menhirs, cromlechs and stone circles, "all belonging to dead religions and forgotten tribes of men."

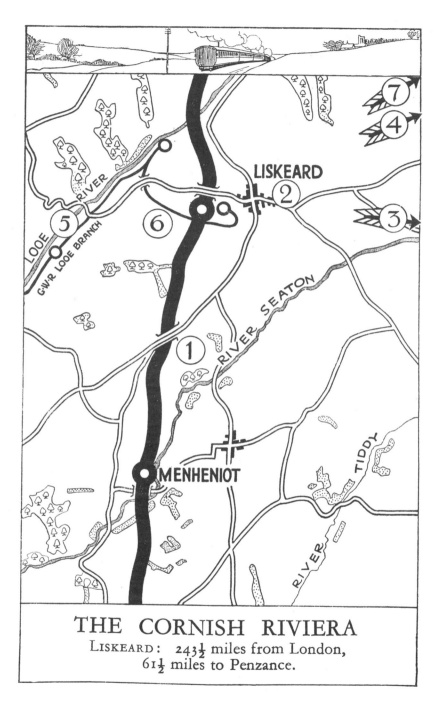

THE CORNISH RIVIERA

LISKEARD: 243½ miles from London,
61½ miles to Penzance.

LISKEARD TO LEWARNE

Near Doublebois

THE tower of St. Cleer Church (1) rising out of the landscape about two and a half miles to the north, makes a landmark to the right as we run clear of Liskeard, with the main road to Bodmin keeping us fairly close company on the same side. Rail and road soon enter the valley of the River Fowey (2) and the three run close together for the next five miles.

The charming river, flowing between well-wooded banks, joins us close to Doublebois (3), a district rich in those Runic crosses with intricate interlaced patterns which form a remarkable chapter in Cornish archæology. At this point, too, the river is itself joined by a tributary that comes down from the north through another wooded vale and flows close to Treverbyn Vean (4) seen on the right of the line just beyond the meeting of the two streams at the point appropriately named Two Waters Foot (5). The house, which is the home of Mrs. Cocks, is a modern one, but the lord of the manor of Treverbyn is required by ancient custom to present a grey cloak to the Duke of Cornwall whenever he crosses the border from Devon into Cornwall.

River Fowey

A couple of miles across country to the left, beyond the lovely Larynn Woods (6), which clothe the Fowey Valley on that side, is Braddock Down (7), the scene of a battle fought on January 19th, 1643, between a Royalist force led by Sir Ralph Hopton and Sir Bevil Grenville and a portion of the Roundhead garrison of Plymouth, which had marched out here under Ruthven, the governor of the port for the Parliament. In this engagement the Royalists won a decisive victory.

To the north of the line opposite Larynn Woods are the woods round about Lewarne, and Lewarne House (8), the seat of Mr. Allan Campbell, will be seen amid a setting of trees.

On each side of the railway, dotting the hillsides are the barrows, (or burial mounds) entrenchments and earthworks (9) both of the Stone Age men and of the Celts who succeeded them. The strip of hilly country between the railway and the scene of Braddock fight is marked at frequent stages by these evidences of the very early occupation of Cornwall.

Near Lewarne

The River Fowey, which the railway now follows so closely for several miles, is one of the most delightful of Cornish streams, coming down from the highlands of Bodmin Moor and giving itself to the sea at the attractive little coast resort which bears its own name.

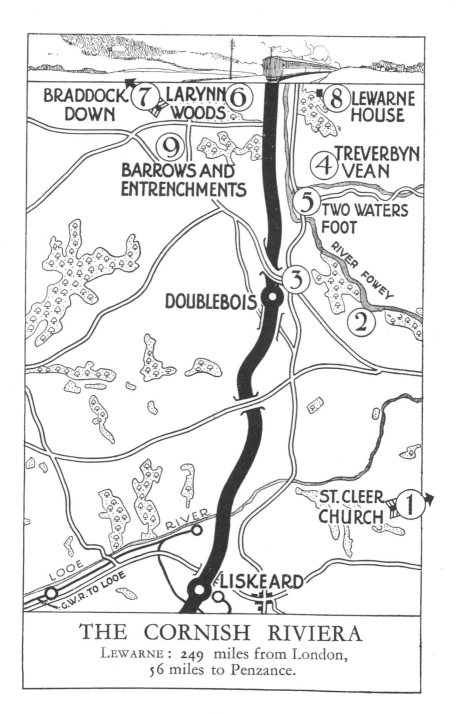

BRADDOCK DOWN ⑦ LARYNN ⑥ WOODS ⑧ LEWARNE HOUSE

⑨ BARROWS AND ENTRENCHMENTS

④ TREVERBYN VEAN

⑤ TWO WATERS FOOT

RIVER FOWEY

③ DOUBLEBOIS

②

① ST. CLEER CHURCH

RIVER

LOOE

G.W.R. TO LOOE

LISKEARD

THE CORNISH RIVIERA

LEWARNE : 249 miles from London,
56 miles to Penzance.

LEWARNE TO RESTORMEL

The Edge of the Moors

HALF-A-MILE or so beyond Lewarne a little stream finds its way through WELL WOOD (1) and runs into the Fowey which has in the meantime passed under the main road, now between us and the river for about three miles. The valley is still well wooded where the railway curves through it, but beyond the woods are bare open downs—HOLTROAD DOWNS (2) and TAWNA DOWNS (3) on the right, HALL DOWNS (4) and PENKESTLE DOWNS (5) on the left. Holtroad Downs separate Well Wood from the next valley, marked by REDRICE WOOD (6), which sends another little stream into the Fowey. Then CABILLA WOODS (7) are seen where Tawna Downs yield to the valley, and in less than half-a-mile two other tributaries have joined the Fowey.

Now the river is gradually swerving round to south on its way to the coast, and as we bend round with it, GLYNN HOUSE (8), the seat of the Vivyan family, is seen on the right just before the main road which has kept us company from Liskeard takes its farewell and turns off to the right for Bodmin. A few hundred yards farther on is BODMIN ROAD STATION (9), where an important branch line strikes off to the right for Bodmin and Wade-bridge—important because Bodmin, although a town of less than 6,000 population, is the county town of Cornwall.

The Moors

Bodmin lies about three miles across country to the north-west of Bodmin Road Station. It is a place of high antiquity, and although most of its numerous mediæval chapels and other buildings have long since disappeared, sufficient relics remain to make the town very interesting as a point of research for those who wish to pursue the fascinating subject of Cornish history.

Passing through the short BROWN QUEEN TUNNEL (10) and curving round through the wooded valley, still keeping close beside the river, we come in another mile or so to where the magnificent ruins of RESTORMEL CASTLE (11) stand, almost hidden by trees, on top of a prominent rise, with the modern Restormel House close by. The castle, which has now been in ruins for many centuries, is believed to have been built by the Cardenham

Restormel Castle

family in the time of Edward I. It was at one time the residence of the Earls of Cornwall, and now forms part of the property attached to the Duchy of Cornwall. Opposite Restormel, DRUIDS HILL (12), with a cross on its summit and woods clothing its slopes, is seen across country to the left a mile distant.

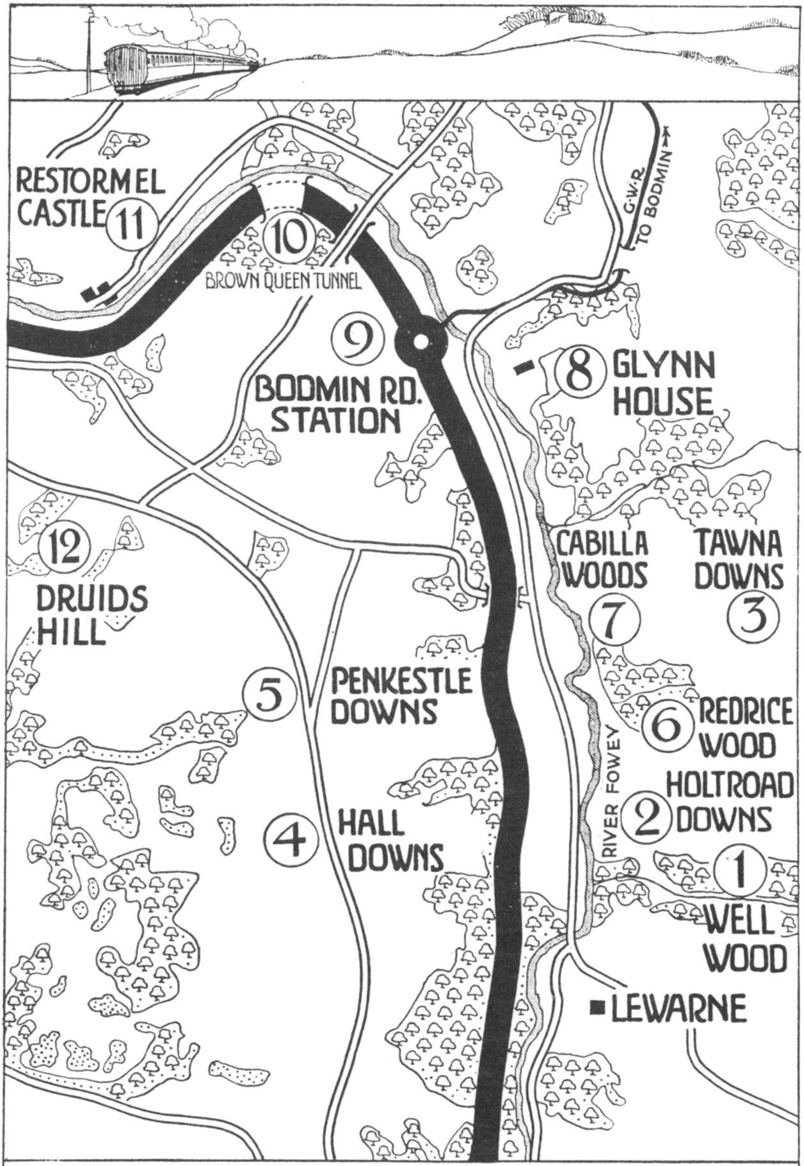
G.W.R. TO BODMIN
RESTORMEL CASTLE 11
10
BROWN QUEEN TUNNEL
9
BODMIN RD. STATION
8 GLYNN HOUSE
12
DRUIDS HILL
CABILLA WOODS
TAWNA DOWNS
7
3
5
PENKESTLE DOWNS
6 REDRICE WOOD
RIVER FOWEY
HOLTROAD DOWNS
2
4
HALL DOWNS
1
WELL WOOD
LEWARNE

THE CORNISH RIVIERA

Bodmin Road: 252½ miles from London, 52½ miles to Penzance.

RESTORMEL TO PAR

Druids Hill

AS the line bends round the castle-crowned headland of Restormel, DRUIDS' HILL (1) is still the most notable thing about the landscape to the left of us. The name of it is significant and neighbouring burial grounds and entrenchments show that it was at least familiar ground to people of the Druid age.

A mile beyond Restormel is the ancient town of LOSTWITHIEL (2) lying in the valley of the Fowey. The most plausible of many explanations of the quaint name is that it means " Lost-within-the-hill "—a fairly good description if one comes to the town by, say, the road across the moors from Liskeard to St. Austell. At one moment, no town in sight for miles and miles ; at the next, Lostwithiel lies spread out at one's feet. But the railway approach has less of this element of surprise ; we are already in the valley and the smoke of the little town is seen ahead soon after passing Restormel. In the parish church, which exhibits an octagonal lantern tower, a queer ceremony is said to have been performed in 1644. A party of Roundheads, contemptuous alike of Church and King, brought a horse into the church and foolishly christened it " Charles " at the ancient font which is still in use.

Lostwithiel

Lostwithiel is a junction of some importance, for here the FOWEY BRANCH (3) bears off to the left and follows the river down its estuary. The main line crosses the river and then takes farewell of the Fowey valley and strikes across the moors on a short cut to the coast.

Beyond TREVERRAN TUNNEL (4) the line traverses a district devoted to china clay mining, now the chief industry of Cornwall save for agriculture. Great cone-shaped dumps of clay look rather like pyramids in the distance, and all the streams are white, as though flowing with milk instead of water.

The tower of TYWARDREATH CHURCH (5) now appears on the left, standing almost on the same spot as a Benedictine priory which gave the place importance in mediæval times. Beyond the village is TRENYTHON HOUSE (6) set high up amid woodlands. On the other side of the line the mining village of ST. BLAZEY (7)

Gribben Head. Nr Par

is seen with the tower of its granite church rising out of the smoke. At PAR STATION (8) a branch which goes to St. Blazey and right across Cornwall to Newquay leaves the main line. St. Blazey is named after the famous Bishop Blaize, patron saint of woolcombers. whose festival is kept here on Feb. 3rd.

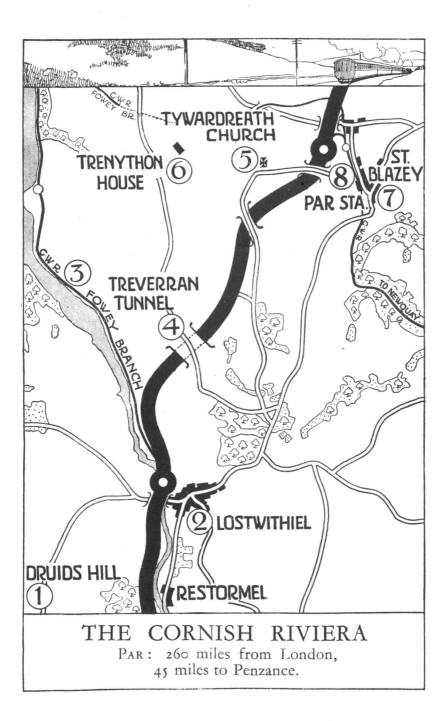

TYWARDREATH
CHURCH

TRENYTHON
HOUSE ⑥

⑤

ST.
BLAZEY
⑧
PAR STA. ⑦

TO NEWQUAY

C.W.R.
FOWEY BR.

C.W.R. FOWEY BRANCH

③

TREVERRAN
TUNNEL
④

LOSTWITHIEL
②

DRUIDS HILL
①

RESTORMEL

THE CORNISH RIVIERA

PAR: 260 miles from London,
45 miles to Penzance.

PAR TO ST. AUSTELL

China Clay District

THE outstanding feature of the country through which we are now passing is the China Clay Industry, of which evidences appear on all sides. This interesting Cornish industry plays a considerable part in English commerce. Not only are thousands of tons of the fine white clay despatched every year to the Potteries district, but large consignments are also sent to Lancashire, where the clay is used as a chemical ingredient in the manufacture of calico, and from the port of Fowey, where the Great Western Railway Co. has installed electrical loading machinery, it is shipped all over the world.

The rich deposit of Cornish china clay was discovered in 1763, and Josiah Wedgwood played a great part in pioneering the industry by leasing some clay mines near St. Austell.

Just beyond Par Station we skirt the edge of PAR SANDS (1) and PAR HARBOUR (2) which is busy with the export of china clay and gives us a peep of picturesque shipping at its quays. Beyond it we have a view of the sea at ST. AUSTELL BAY (3).

For a mile or more now we are riding close to the sea, and looking across the bay near Par Harbour gain a good view of GRIBBIN HEAD (4), which juts out into the Channel between the mouth of the Fowey and St. Austell Bay. Fowey is out of sight just round the corner to the east. The corresponding promontory

Black Head

on the western extremity of the bay is BLACK HEAD (5). The two headlands are just four miles apart.

Looking inland, the modern steepled church of ST. BLAZEY GATE (6), a village on the road from St. Blazey to St. Austell, is seen, while at a clearing of the woods a little further west TRE-GREHAN HOUSE (7), the seat of the Carlyon family, comes into view. The countryside carries very little timber here, compared with what we saw in the Fowey Valley, but the belt of trees by Tregrehan stretches south and extends to the opposite side of the railway.

In this part of Cornwall we have not only the modern and prosperous china clay industry, but also many reminders of the ancient copper mining industry. The church-like towers in

St. Austell Church

ruinous condition noticed from time to time on the hill-tops mark deserted pit shafts. After passing St. Blazey Gate the railway gradually draws away from the sea as it approaches ST. AUSTELL (8) the chief centre of the china clay industry. Its great granite church on the left is one of the most ornate in Cornwall.

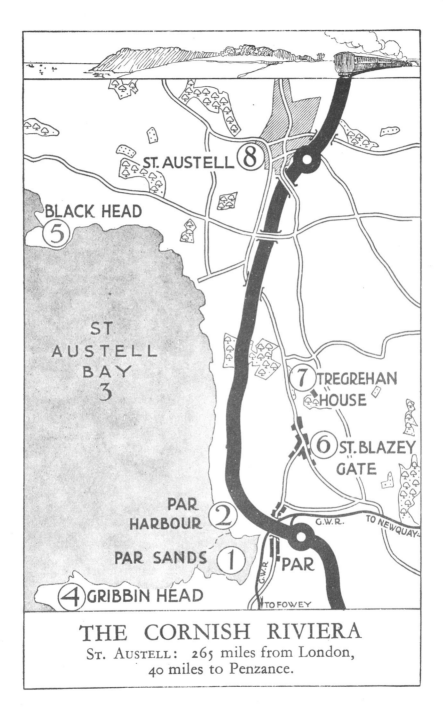

ST. AUSTELL 8

BLACK HEAD
5

ST
AUSTELL
BAY
3

7 TREGREHAN
HOUSE

6 ST. BLAZEY
GATE

PAR
HARBOUR 2

PAR SANDS 1

G.W.R. TO NEWQUAY

G.W.R. PAR

4 GRIBBIN HEAD

TO FOWEY

THE CORNISH RIVIERA

St. Austell: 265 miles from London,
40 miles to Penzance.

ST. AUSTELL TO GRAMPOUND ROAD

China Clay Dumps

BEYOND St. Austell, the line skirts the edge of SPARNON MOOR (1) which banks up on the right to the west of a small milky rivulet, which we cross about a mile out of the town. We are still in the heart of the china clay district, and BURNGULLOW COMMON (2), rising to a height of 663 feet immediately beyond Sparnon Moor is conspicuous chiefly on account of its huge dumps of china clay, although its old-time significance was that of a beacon.

We are at close quarters with some extensive china clay works beside the line on the right just before reaching BURNGULLOW STATION (3).

The round mound which rises within a few yards of the line on the left hand side rather less than a mile beyond the station is an earthwork known as TRETHULLEN CASTLE (4) but presents nothing in the way of ruins. Just beyond here, on the opposite side, a picturesque old WATER MILL (5) with a huge wheel as high as the building itself, is worked by the small stream—a tributary of the Fal—running almost parallel with the railway for a couple of miles or more.

Now we cross the RIVER FAL (6), and its widening valley breaks the bareness of the moorlands with a charming patch of woodland on the farther bank. On the right of the line is TRENOWTH WOOD (7) containing remains of ancient chapels, while to the left is the smaller TREVAN WOOD (8).

China Clay Dumps

Do you notice what a lot of place-names in Cornwall begin with " Tre ? " No less than 224 towns, villages and hamlets in the county start their names in this fashion, to say nothing of woods, farms and other small points of the landscape which have the same characteristic. The reason for this is that in the ancient Cornish language " tre " meant a homestead or town-place.

The contours of a prehistoric CAMP (9) are seen on a hill to the left just before passing through GRAMPOUND ROAD STATION (10). The station is two miles distant from the once-upon-a-time town and now quiet village of GRAMPOUND (11) which lies at the point where the Fal is crossed by the main road from St. Austell to Truro.

The Water Mill

The place, now having a population of less than 500, was formerly a 'rotten borough" and returned two Members of Parliament until 1821, when it was disfranchised for corrupt practices. The name is a corruption of grand pont (great bridge) which refers, of course, to the important bridge over the Fal here.

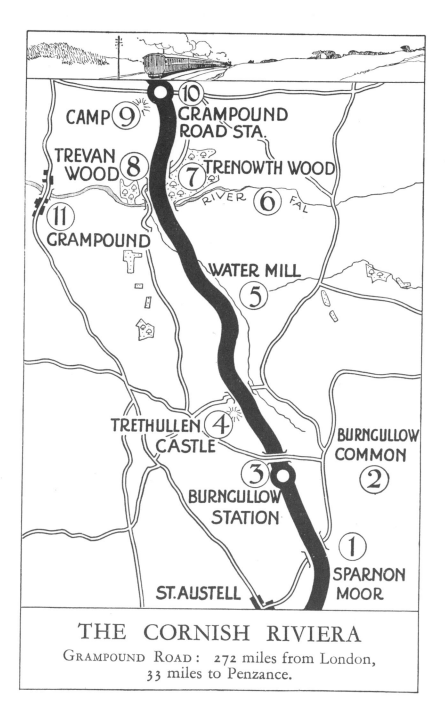

CAMP ⑨

TREVAN WOOD ⑧

⑪ GRAMPOUND

⑩ GRAMPOUND ROAD STA.

⑦ TRENOWTH WOOD

RIVER FAL ⑥

WATER MILL ⑤

TRETHULLEN CASTLE ④

BURNGULLOW STATION ③

BURNGULLOW COMMON ②

ST. AUSTELL

① SPARNON MOOR

THE CORNISH RIVIERA

Grampound Road: 272 miles from London,
33 miles to Penzance.

GRAMPOUND ROAD TO TRURO

Probus
Church

IN a couple of miles we draw level with the noble tower of PROBUS CHURCH (1) on the left, said to be the tallest and most beautiful in Cornwall and characteristic of the late Perpendicular period.

The church is dedicated to St. Probus and St. Grace. In 1851 a reliquary containing two skulls was discovered beneath the altar, and it is believed that these skulls are none other than those of the patron saints of this ancient church, which was of sufficient importance to be made a collegiate church in A.D. 926. The reliquary and skulls are preserved in the north chapel.

Probus parish, which runs down to the Fal on the east, contains an ancient ENTRENCHMENT (2) close to the farmhouse called Golden, and there are other earthworks near at hand.

To the right of the line, the MAIN ROAD (3) from Bodmin, the legal capital of Cornwall, to Truro, possessing many claims to be considered the real centre of Cornish life, comes down the valley from LADOCK (4) in close company with the TRESILLIAN RIVER (5), and after running alongside the railway for a short distance passes under it just beyond PROBUS AND LADOCK HALT (6).

The
Summer
House

The pleasant strip of woodland which runs down to the railway a little farther along on the right is part of the TREHANE ESTATE (7), and the short frontage of trees it presents to the railway provides the background for a picturesque little SUMMER HOUSE (8) built by a former owner of Trehane who, in the days when the railway was still a novelty in Cornwall, made this his favourite spot from which to watch the passing of the incredible locomotive and its string of open trucks.

Now the train speeds through POLPERRO TUNNEL (9) and BUCKSHEAD TUNNEL (10) which presumably owes its name to some hunting incident of bygone days. On emerging from it, TRURO (11) is seen immediately ahead to the left, the three lofty towers of its magnificent cathedral dominating the city. This great building—the first Gothic cathedral completed in England since the Reformation—was begun in 1880 and the exterior finished in 1912. We have glimpses of the navigable TRURO

Nearing Truro

RIVER (12) in passing through the town, as well as of the large Wesleyan College on a hill to the left, and the church tower of KENWYN (13) to the right overlooking Lys Escop, the residence of the Bishop of Truro. The big modern house close by Truro Station is Trevinnard Court, now used as the Cathedral choir school.

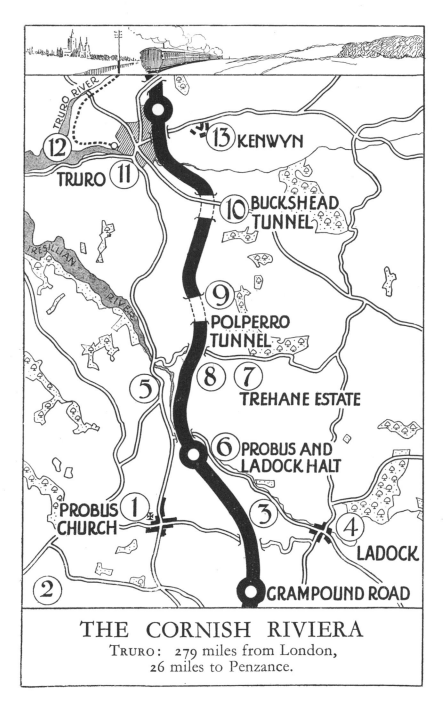

THE CORNISH RIVIERA

TRURO: 279 miles from London,
26 miles to Penzance.

Map labels:
12
13 KENWYN
TRURO 11
10 BUCKSHEAD TUNNEL
9
POLPERRO TUNNEL
5 8 7
TREHANE ESTATE
6 PROBUS AND LADOCK HALT
PROBUS CHURCH 1
3
4
LADOCK
2
GRAMPOUND ROAD

TRURO RIVER
TRESILLIAN RIVER

TRURO TO CHACEWATER

A glimpse of Truro River

AS the train draws out of Truro (1) there is a view looking down the Truro River (2) which carries to the Fal about three miles to the south-east the combined waters of two smaller rivers—the Allan and the Kenwyn—already crossed by us and which meet at the city.

The Falmouth branch (3) bears off to the left across Penwithers Viaduct (4), which at the time of writing this book remains as one of the few of the great timber bridges designed by Brunel to carry the railway across the numerous valleys that break up the Cornish landscape. Almost all the way from Plymouth we have been crossing viaducts at every mile or so—substantial structures of stone arches. Originally they were all built of wood like this picturesque viaduct of Penwithers, soon to be replaced by an embankment.

Now we are entering the chief mining district of Cornwall, strewn with the relics of a vanished commercial greatness. Almost every hill carries on its summit one or more disused mine chimneys with engine houses adjoining. When seen at a distance these look very much like church towers. The landscape is also dotted with old mine shafts, ringed by low walls or embankments to prevent people falling into them.

Near Truro

The main road (5) from Truro to Redruth presently crosses the railway, coming across hills that are thickly strewn with prehistoric burial grounds and encampments. The long Cornish peninsula narrows in quickly as we fly westward, and from this stage of the journey to the end we are never more than half a dozen miles from the sea and frequently come within sight of it, swinging over first to one coast and then to the other.

At Chacewater (6) whose modern church tower rises to the left, we are but four miles from the north coast of Cornwall—we should strike it a little to the south of St. Agnes' Head if we went forward as the crow flies. Chacewater has its place in the history of engineering, for it was in a mine here that Watt's first pumping engine was erected.

A little way beyond Chacewater station, the Newquay branch

Nr. Chacewater

(7) bears off to the right, passing almost immediately through the hamlet of Blackwater (8) on its way to St. Agnes and Perranporth, after which it manœuvres its roundabout course through downs to the charming seaside resort farther north. There is a whole cluster of tumuli (9) north east of Black-water.

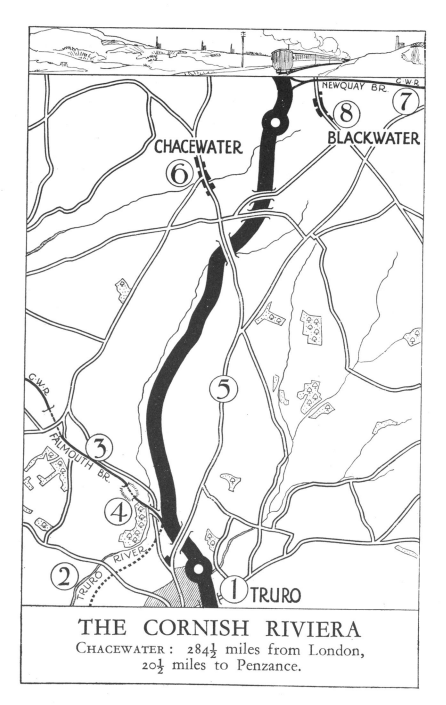

NEWQUAY BR.

G.W.R.

⑦

⑧

CHACEWATER

BLACKWATER

⑥

⑤

C.W.R.

FALMOUTH BR.

③

④

TRURO RIVER

②

① TRURO

THE CORNISH RIVIERA

CHACEWATER: $284\frac{1}{2}$ miles from London,
$20\frac{1}{2}$ miles to Penzance.

CHACEWATER TO CARN BREA

Near Scorrier

BEYOND the junction with the New-quay branch, the main line bends south and SCORRIER (1) gives us a fine plantation of pines to vary the rather bare aspect of the neighbouring hillsides. The MAIN ROAD (2) running alongside the woodland is the Truro-Redruth road which we crossed about four miles back.

Through the woods lies the modern mansion of SCORRIER HOUSE (3)

Here we may take preliminary note of the fact that the striking hill which is seen ahead, now on the right, now on the left as the railway serpentines through the landscape, is Carn Brea, concerning which we shall have more to say when we come closer to it.

Meanwhile, ST. AGNES BEACON (4) rising to a height of 629 feet just inland from St. Agnes Head, is seen about four miles across country to the right, and on the same side a sudden gap in the hills gives us a charming glimpse of the sea three miles away at PORTREATH (5), a tiny port of the North Cornish coast.

In the middle distance is the mining village of ILLOGAN (6) whose church tower set on a hill serves as a useful landmark to mariners. We shall have a better view of Illogan after passing through REDRUTH (7) one of the chief mining centres of Cornwall, which we are now rapidly approaching.

Mines at Redruth

Redruth presents us with the industrial aspect of Cornish life, with its iron foundries and tin smelting works, while the surrounding countryside is heavily scored with tin and copper mines. In the town is the house in which gas was used for lighting for the first time in England as the invention of William Murdock. That was in 1792, and an inscription on the house, which was Murdock's home, credits him with having made and tested the first locomotive here in 1784.

Half a mile out of the town, is REDRUTH PARISH CHURCH (8), but here we have eyes for little else than the spectacular summit of CARN BREA (9). The line passes round the foot of this rocky hill, which now appears on the left. Many relics of Stone Age men have been found on Carn Brea, which was one of the great fortified places of Cornwall in pre-Roman days, long before the

Carn Brea

erection of the CASTLE (10), whose remains are visible amid the crags of the peak. The MONUMENT (11) in the form of a Celtic cross commemorates Lord de Dunstanville. Just after rounding the hill we pass through CARN BREA STATION (12). The hill remains in sight for sometime after passing it.

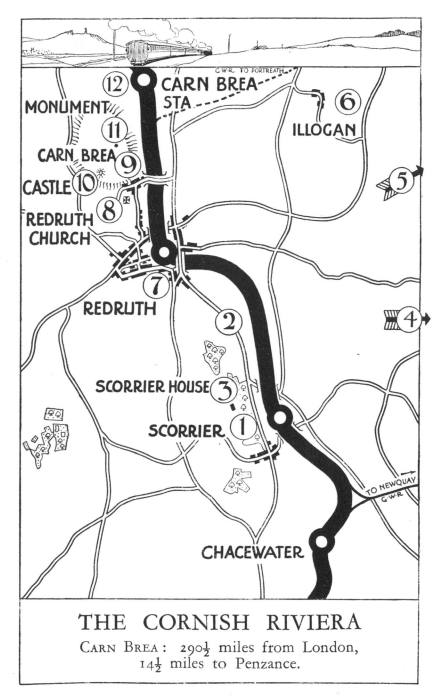

GWR TO PORTREATH

TO NEWQUAY
G.W.R.

THE CORNISH RIVIERA

CARN BREA: 290½ miles from London,
14½ miles to Penzance.

CARN BREA TO HAYLE

Godolphin & Tregonning Hills

CLOSE to the railway on the right soon after passing Carn Brea Station are the surface works of the famous DOLCOATH MINE (1)—one of the richest of the Cornish tin and copper mines before the industry fell on evil days. It is nearly 3,000 feet deep. The church tower seen a little farther away is the modern one of TUCKINGMILL (2) Behind it the landscape yields itself to CAMBORNE PLANTATION (3) and other woodlands which stretch almost to the coast, less than three miles distant from us now.

CAMBORNE (4) is a mining town of much the same character as Redruth. Half-a-dozen miles away to the left rise the peaks of GODOLPHIN HILL (5) and TREGINNING HILL (6), the former 582 feet and the latter 635 feet at the summit. On the top of Treginning Hill are the remains of Castle Pencaire, and the lines of prehistoric encampments break its slopes, but these show up less prominently than the numerous mine-heads and china clay works scattered about both this hill and its neighbour Godolphin.

Another landmark on this side on the sky-line about three miles away is CROWAN CHURCH (7). There is a good view of this just before reaching GWINEAR ROAD STATION (8) where a BRANCH LINE (9) turns off to the south for Helston and the Lizard district.

Nr. Camborne

Cornwall has often been likened to a leg—or, by a clever G.W.R. poster, to the shape of Italy in reverse. The leg ends in a foot, with a well-defined toe and heel. The Lizard is the heel—Land's End is the toe. We are travelling at the moment somewhere on the instep.

GWINEAR CHURCH (10) shows up on the left soon after the station is passed, while the hills of the Land's End district are seen twenty miles or so away as we look straight ahead from the left side of the train. The curious formation of sandhills, rather like the dunes of the Belgian coast, which now appear only about a mile away to the right are the TOWANS (11) which border ST. IVES BAY (12), while the buildings of an EXPLOSIVES FACTORY (13) stand out prominently in the same direction.

Sandhills, or 'Towans'

Sand is a force to be reckoned with in this part of Cornwall. Owing to its encroachment PHILLACK CHURCH (14), which we see in the middle distance, had to be rebuilt, except for the tower, in 1857. The busy port of HAYLE (15), with its iron foundries and a modern church lies immediately ahead.

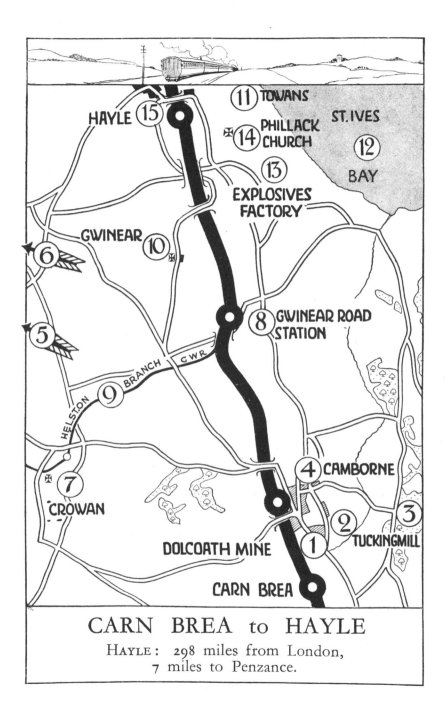

CARN BREA to HAYLE

HAYLE: 298 miles from London,
7 miles to Penzance.

HAYLE TO MARAZION

St Ives Bay.

FROM the broad estuary of the HAYLE RIVER (1) rise two lofty towers of steel girder work carrying electric mains across the river. Through this break in the landscape we have a good view into ST. IVES BAY (2) with a passing glimpse of the picturesque old town of ST. IVES (3) the haunt of a whole School of artists three or four miles away.

A hill which rises half-way between us and St. Ives shows on its summit what looks, from a distance, like a church steeple, but is really the KNILL MONUMENT (4) erected by an eccentric lawyer in 1782. He left a bequest payable every five years to ten girls from the neighbouring town who should climb the hill and sing the 100th Psalm at his monument.

> "There was an old lawyer named Knill,
> Who left a peculiar will;
> Ten girls from St. Ives
> Have the time of their lives
> For singing on top of his hill."

On the western bank of the Hayle estuary rises the fine tower of LELANT CHURCH (5), and in the churchyard are four ancient crosses of the peculiar Cornish type. The famous WEST CORNWALL GOLF LINKS (6) lie just to the north of the village.

CARNSEW RESERVOIR (7) is part of Hayle Harbour. Water is stored here at high tide and frequently allowed to escape with a rush in order to scour the harbour channel.

Lelant & Knill Monument

At ST. ERTH STATION (8), with fine palms growing upon it as a reminder that we are now on the Cornish Riviera, the ST. IVES BRANCH (9) turns off *via* Lelant. ST. ERTH VILLAGE (10) lies about half-a-mile from the railway on the left. Sub-tropical plants flourish in its churchyard, which also contains a remarkable cross mingling Saxon with ancient Irish ornament.

A mile or so across country to the right is TRENCROM HILL (11), whose rugged summit figures in Cornish mythology as the home of giants. Farther away, and a little to the left of Trencrom, rises the greater height of CASTLE-AN-DINAS HILL (12), having on its summit a tower, or "folly" of modern erection.

Ludgvan Church

LUDGVAN VILLAGE (13), with a 14th century church tower, soon appears on the right, set astride the road from Hayle to Penzance. Ludgvan's claim to fame rests in the fact that the last native wolf in England is said to have been killed in this parish. In another mile we strike the coast at MARAZION (14).

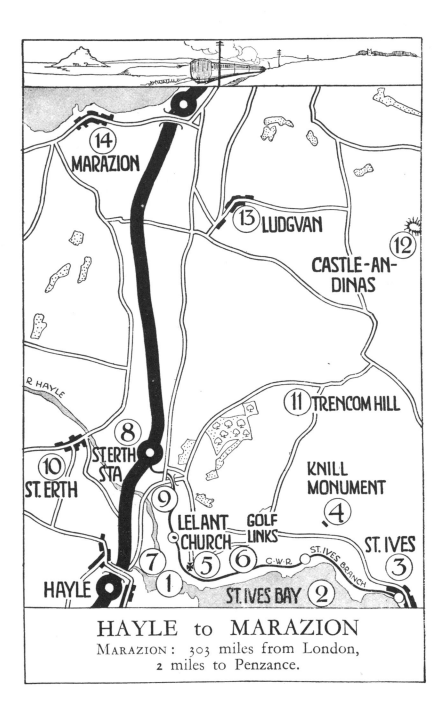

14 MARAZION

13 LUDGVAN

12

CASTLE-AN-DINAS

R HAYLE

11 TRENCOM HILL

8 ST ERTH STA

KNILL MONUMENT

10 ST. ERTH

9

LELANT CHURCH

GOLF LINKS

4

ST. IVES

7

5

6

G.W.R.

ST. IVES BRANCH

3

HAYLE

1

ST. IVES BAY

2

HAYLE to MARAZION

MARAZION: 303 miles from London,
2 miles to Penzance.

MARAZION TO PENZANCE

Mounts Bay

WHILE approaching MARAZION **(1)** we have caught a glimpse of that almost incredible sight when seen for the first time—ST. MICHAEL'S MOUNT **(2)** towering up from Mount's Bay. In the first flood of enthusiasm for one of the most wonderful pictures on the coasts of Britain we feel the whole journey would have been worth while if it gave us no more than this. On the pinnacle of rock 230 feet above the sea a monastery was established before the Norman Conquest. The castle which now crowns the Mount is the seat of Lord St. Levan. For most of the day and night the sea divides the Mount from Marazion, its nearest neighbour on the mainland, but at each tide it is possible to cross over on the sands during a period of about four hours.

We are now but a couple of miles from the journey's end. Already Penzance is seen almost straight ahead, while a little to the left of it appears NEWLYN **(3)**, a charming little resort on the tiny bay called GWAVAS LAKE **(4)**, and behind it and to the left rise the hills which stretch westwards towards LAND'S END **(5)**.

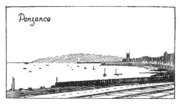

Penzance

To the south of Newlyn the small ST. CLEMENT'S ISLE **(6)** stands a little way out to sea in front of MOUSEHOLE **(7)**, and the church of PAUL **(8)** is seen on the sky-line. Drawing nearer to Penzance we may look back across the broad sweep of Mount's Bay to the LIZARD **(9)** and the tall wireless masts at Poldhu.

And now PENZANCE **(10)** and the end of the journey—an almost incredible journey it seems, for we were in London this morning and now, at five o'clock in the afternoon, we find ourselves within a few miles of Land's End. Good gracious ! how the time flies ! —which is but another way of saying how the " 10.30 Limited " flies !

Penzance groups itself finely above the sea, with houses rising in irregular stages up to where a great church and domed market house stand on the higher ground. The picturesque shipping of its Harbour, whence sail the boats for the Scilly Isles, greets us immediately on leaving the Station, and the broad Promenade beyond gives glorious views to seaward and for many miles along

Penzance Harbour

the hilly coast of the Cornish Riviera, with St. Michael's Mount away to the left. " The Land's End," says Mr. Harris Stone, " is the land of the wild, the picturesque and the imaginative ; it is the land of giants and romance, the birthplace of stories and children's tales which have achieved impossible fame."

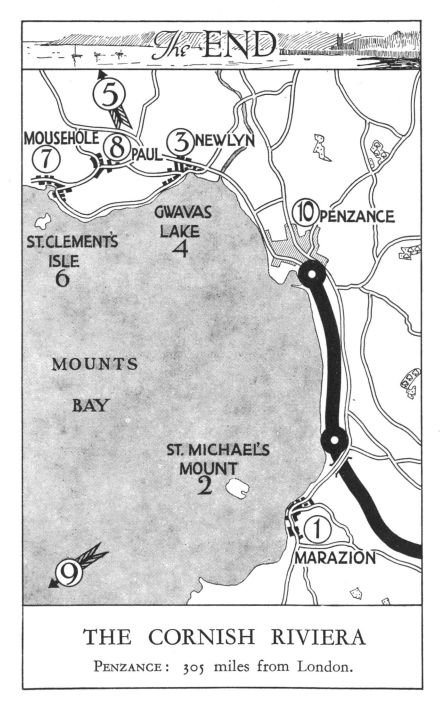

THE CORNISH RIVIERA

Penzance : 305 miles from London.

The first of the many editions of *Through the Window - The Great Western Railway from Paddington to Penzance* was published in 1924 and remained in print for many years. In this facsimile reprint we have added twenty of the GWR Paddington to Penzance pages from Bradshaw's Railway timetable of that time.

LONDON, READING, CHIPPENHAM, WEYMOUTH, and TAUNTON.—Great Western.

Miles	Down.	Week Days.																			
		mrn	mrn	mrn	mrn	mrn	mrn	mrn	mrn	mrn	mrn	mrn	mrn	mrn	mrn	mrn	mrn	mrn	mrn	mrn	mrn
	PADDINGTON ....dep.	1 B 0										5 30		6 30	7 30					7 30	
36	Reading .... "	1B51										6 18		7 53	8 28					8 20	
37	Reading (West)													7 56							
41½	Theale§, for Bradfield College													8 5							
44¾	Aldermaston													8 12							
46½	Midgham													8 18							
49½	Thatcham													8 24							
53	Newbury 56 ....arr.													8 31	8 51						
91½	56 Southampton Town † arr.													1055	10 55						
—	Newbury ....dep.													Stop	8 54						
58½	Kintbury														9 4						
61½	Hungerford														9 12						
66½	Bedwyn														9 22						
70	Savernake ** 59, 122, 123..														9 31						
75½	Pewsey														9 40						
78¾	Woodborough									m				m	9 47		m				m
81	Patney and Chirton									7 25				9 8	9 55		1010				10 7
85¾	Devizes ¶ .... arr.									7 35	m			9 18							10 17
	Devizes ¶ .... dep.									Stop	8 5			Stop	9g40		9f55				10 20
90	Seend ¶										8 19										10 31
87	Lavington																1024				
91½	Edington and Bratton																1035				
—	Miles 12 Oxford 56 .....dep.	3B48													7F10					7 10	
—	12 Didcot 56 ...... "											6 44			7F38					7 43	
—	12 Swindon ...... "	5 35				m						7 35								9 20	
—	— Chippenham ¶ dep.	6 7				7 10						8b25								10b10	
—	6 Melksham ¶	6 22				7 25						8b40								10b27	
94	8¾ Holt ¶	6 32				7 32					8 29	8b47								10b33	10 40
97	11¾ Trowbridge 48, 49 arr.	6 38				7 39					8 36	8b54			10i32					10b40	10 48
100½	49 Bradford-on-Avon arr.	7 19				7 54					8 52	9b9								11 24	11 24
109¾	49 Bath .... "	7 39				8 17					9 16	9b32								11 17	11 17
121¼	49 Bristol (Temple M.) "	8 12				8 50					9 38	1015b		mrn		m				11 40	11 40
—	48 Bristol (Temple M.) dep.			6 0			6 20	7h5				8 15		8 40		9 15				Stop	
—	48 Bath .... "			6 24								8 36				9 45					
—	48 Bradford-on-Avon.. "			6 48						mrn		9 2				1011					
—	Trowbridge ....dep.	6 44		7 4						8 15		9 15				1023					
95½	Westbury 48, 49 ....arr.	6 52		7 12						8 23		9 24			10 16	1032	1044				
120	48 Salisbury ....arr.			8 20								1032									
—	Westbury ....dep.			7 21			Via Durston.			8 28		9 30		Via Durston.	10 21		1048				
101½	Frome 48 .... arr.			7 31	m			8 14		8 38		9 40			10 31		1059				
	Frome 48 .... dep.			7 36	8 0			8 25		Stop		9 42			10 34		11 2				
106½	Witham 41			7 50	8 11			8 42				9 53					1116				
111¾	Bruton ‡			8 0	8 22							10 2	m								
115½	Castle Cary ¶			8 9	8 30							1010	1020								
120	Sparkford			8 19								1020									
122¾	Marston Magna			8 25	Leaves Durston at 9 39 aft.							1026								mrn	
127	Yeovil (Pen Mill) 52 arr.			8 33			8 45			mrn		1034		11 8				m		m	
	Yeovil (Pen Mill) 52 dep.						8 55			9 50		1040						11 15		11 30	
131½	Yetminster						9 5											11 27			
135¾	Evershot						9 17											11 41			
139¾	Maiden Newton 59.. arr.						9 23					11 2						11 49		Leaves Durston at 12 54 aft.	
	Maiden Newton 59.. dep.						9 27					11 5						11 50			
143½	Grimstone and Frampton.						9 34		m									11 57			
147½	Dorchester *¶ 137						9 44		1050			1118						12 7			
152¾	Upwey Junction ¶ 54						9 54		11 2									12 19			
154½	Weymouth (Town)....arr.						10 0		1110			1130						12 27			
120	Keinton Mandeville				8 43								1031								
122¾	Charlton Mackrell				8 50								1037								
125½	Somerton (Somerset)				8 59								1045								
128	Long Sutton and Pitney				9 5								1051								
130	Langport East				9 11								1056								
127½	Yeovil (Town) 163.. arr.									9 52										11 32	
	Yeovil (Town) 163.. dep.		8 0							9 56										11 43	
132½	Montacute		8 11							10 8										11 56	
135	Martock		8 18							1015										12 8	
140	Langport West		8 30							1026										12 18	
135	Athelney		8 41		9 22					1036			11 7		11 18				m	12 20	
137½	Durston 17		8 46		9 27					1041			1115						1147	12 36	
143	Taunton 22, 54 ....arr.		8 59		9 49					1052					11 30				12 0	1 7	
203¾	54 Ilfracombe 144 ....arr.				2 20					2 20					3z50				4 10	4z53	
173¾	22 Exeter (St. David's) "		1019		10 37					1227					12 27					2 19	
199¾	22 Torquay .... "				11 44					1 47					1 47					3 15	
226½	22 Plymouth (Millbay) "				12a16					2a15					2a15					4 19	
305¾	22 Penzance .... "				3 35					5 0					5 0					7 55	

☞ **For Steamers between Weymouth and Guernsey and Jersey, see page 912.**

GREAT WESTERN RAILWAY.

ROYAL HOTEL.

PADDINGTON STATION, London, W.2.

Handsome Reception Rooms, suitable for Wedding Parties, Dinners, Meetings, etc., on Ground Floor.

Table d'Hote, 6-0 to 8-30 p.m. (open to non-residents).   Electric Light throughout.   Lifts.

Telephone : 7000 Paddington.   A complete installation.   Separate telephone in every room.

Telegraphic Address : "Padotel," Rail, London.

Tariff and full particulars can be obtained on application to the Hotel Manager.

Main Line.]   3   **[Great Western.**

LONDON, READING, CHIPPENHAM, WEYMOUTH, and TAUNTON.—Great Western.

Down.																		
	mrn	mrn	mrn	mrn	mrn	mrn	mrn	aft	aft	mrn	mrn	aft	aft	aft	mrn	mrn	noon	aft	aft	aft
PADDINGTON........dep.	....	....	9 0	9 0	10 30	10 30	....	9 0	....	....	....	....	....	1045	10 45	12 0	....	....
Reading................ "	9 32	....	9 50	1012	....	....	....	9 50	....	....	1142	11 48	....	....
Reading (West):........ "	9 35	....	....	1015	....	....	....	....	....	11 51	....
Theale§,forBradfieldCollege	9 44	....	....	1024	....	....	....	....	....	12 0	....
Aldermaston............	9 51	....	....	1031	....	....	....	....	....	12 7	....
Midgham................	9 57	....	....	1037	....	....	....	....	....	12 13	....
Thatcham..............	10 3	....	....	1043	....	....	....	....	....	12 19	....
Newbury 56........arr.	1010	....	....	1050	....	....	....	....	12 6	12 26	....
56 SOUTHAMPTON TOWN † arr.	....	....	....	1 47	....	....	....
Newbury................dep.	1014	....	....	1053	....	....	....	....	12 9	....
Kintbury..............	1024	....	....	11 3	....	....	....	....	1219	....
Hungerford............	1032	....	....	11 9	....	....	....	....	1227	....
Bedwyn................	1042	....	....	....	....	....	....	1237	....
Savernake** 59, 122, 123.	1050	....	....	....	....	....	....	1246	....
Pewsey................	1059	....	....	....	....	....	....	1255	....
Woodborough	11 6	....	....	....	....	....	....	1 2	....	....	111
Patney and Chirton....	1113	....	....	....	....	....	....	1 8	....	....	1 30
Devizes ¶ { arr.	1121	....	....	....	....	....	....	1 16	....
{ dep.	1137	....	....	....	....	....	....	1 18	....	....	12g33
Seend ¶	1147	....	....	....	....	....	....	1 27	....
Lavington.............	....	....	....	....	....	....	....	....	....	1 44
Edington and Bratton..	....	....	....	....	....	....	....	....	....	1 54
12 OXFORD 56........dep.	....	....	9 35	....	....	9 35	....	....	....
12 DIDCOT 56.......... "	....	....	1020	....	....	10 20	....	....	....
12 SWINDON .... "	....	....	1057	....	....	11 15	....	....	....
Chippenham ¶ ....dep.	....	....	1128	....	....	11 50	....	....	....
Melksham ¶	....	....	....	....	....	12 3	....	....	....
Holt ¶	1155	....	....	....	....	12 9	....	1 35	....
Trowbridge 48, 49 . arr.	12 1	....	1148	....	1225	12 15	....	1 41	....
49 BRADFORD-ON-AVON arr.	1254	....	....	....	1254	12 54	....	1 08	....
49 BATH................ "	1 17	....	....	....	....	1 17	....	2 17	....
49 BRISTOL (Temple M.) "	1 47	....	....	....	....	1 47	....	2 54	....
48 BRISTOL(Temple M.)dep.	10 10	1045	....	....	11 40	12c35	....	1 5
48 BATH................ "	10 32	11 6	....	....	12 1	12 59	....	1 26
48 BRADFORD-ON-AVON "	10 58	1124	....	....	12 17	....	1 52
Trowbridge........dep	11 12	1137	1152	....	12 19	12 30	1 24	2 6
Westbury 48, 49 . arr.	11 20	1145	12 0	....	12k8	12 27	12 38	1 32	2 14	2 3
48 SALISBURY........ arr.	12 24	....	....	....	1 28	2 20	3 0
Westbury.............dep.	....	....	....	....	12 12	12 50	....
Frome 48 .... { arr.	....	....	....	....	12 21	1 0	....
{ dep.	....	....	....	....	12 24	1235	1 3	....
Witham 41.............	....	....	....	....	1251	1 14	....
Bruton ¡	....	....	....	....	1 23	111
Castle Cary ¶	....	....	....	....	1 31	1 38	....
Sparkford............	....	....	....	....	1 40	....
Marston Magna........	....	....	....	....	1 46	....
Yeovil (Pen Mill) { arr.	....	....	....	12 56	1 54	....	....	2 25
52 { dep.	....	....	....	12 59	1 59	....
Yetminster..........	....	....	....	....	2 9	....
Evershot............	....	....	....	....	2 21	....
Maiden Newton 59. { arr.	....	....	....	1 21	2 27	....
{ dep.	....	....	....	1 24	2 29	aft
Grinstone and Frampton	....	....	....	....	2 36	111
Dorchester • ¶ 137....	....	....	....	1 38	2 3	2 45	3 25	....
Upwey Junction ¶ 54..	....	....	....	2 15	2 54	3 37	....
Weymouth (Town).. arr.	....	....	....	1 50	2 23	3 0	3 45	....
Keinton Mandeville....	....	....	....	....	1 50	....
Charlton Mackrell....	....	....	....	....	2 11	....
Somerton (Somerset) ..	....	....	....	....	2 19	....
Long Sutton and Pitney	....	....	....	....	2 25	....
Langport East........	....	....	....	....	2 30	....
Yeovil (Town) 163.. { arr.	....	....	....	....	....	2 27
{ dep.	....	....	....	....	....	2 36
Montacute............	....	....	....	....	....	2 45
Martock	....	....	....	....	....	2 55
Langport West........	....	....	....	....	....	3 6
Athelney.............	....	....	....	....	2 41	....	3 16
Durston 17...........	....	....	....	....	2 56	....	3 21
Taunton 22, 54 .... arr.	....	....	1258	....	2 56	....	3 35
54 ILFRACOMBE 144 .. "	....	....	4k10	....	....	6r44	8r10
22 EXETER (St. David's) "	....	....	1k30	....	....	3 0	4 30
22 TORQUAY........... "	....	....	2k46	....	....	3 40	5 48
22 PLYMOUTH (Millbay) "	....	....	2c57	....	....	4c48	6 25
22 PENZANCE.......... "	....	....	....	....	....	7 55	1010

For Notes, see page 6   for Continuation of Trains, see pages 4 to 6.

Bradshaw's General Railway and Steam Navigation Guide

George Bradshaw's surname was synonymous with railway timetables for more than 120 years. During the 1820s he founded the printing firm which became Henry Blacklock & Co. It specialised in engravings and maps including maps of canals and then the early railways. By the end of the 1830s Bradshaw was publishing railway timetable leaflets and by 1841 was producing the monthly Bradshaw's Railway Guide which showed railway timetables for the whole of the country and

London, &c., to Weymouth and Taunton.]   4   [Great Western

LONDON, READING, CHIPPENHAM, WEYMOUTH, and TAUNTON.—Great Western.

Down. — Week Days—*Continued.*

Station										
PADDINGTON .... dep.	mrn 1045	mrn 1120	aft 12 30	...	1 102	0 1 35	2 0	...	2 45	3 15 3 18
Reading .... "	1138	1250	1 18	...	2 102	49 3	3 ...	2 49	3 21	3 59 4 38
Reading (West)	...	1255	...	...	...	3 6	...			4 41
Theale, for Bradfield College	1 4	...	...	2 20	3 15	...			4 30
Aldermaston	1 11	...	...	2 27	3 22	...			4 57
Midgham	1 17	...	...	2 33	3 28	...			5 3
Thatcham	1 23	...	...	2 39	3 34	...			5 9
Newbury 56 .... arr.	1 30	1 42	...	2 46	3 41	...	3 54		5 16
56 SOUTHAMPTON TOWN ‡ arr.	3 41	3 41	...	5 50	...	5 50		
Newbury .... dep.	Stop	1 45	1 522	49	Stop	3 57	4 17	5 19
Kintbury		2 22	59		4 27	5 29
Hungerford		2 103	5		4 10	4 35	5 37
Bedwyn		2 20			4 45	5 47
Savernake** 59, 122, 123	Car to Westbury.	2 29 Stop			4 54	5 54
Pewsey		2 39			5 3	
Woodborough		2 46			5 10	Stop
Patney and Chirton		3 0			5 17	
Devizes ‡ { arr.		2 43			4 41	5 25
{ dep.					4 44	5 30
Seend ‡						5 39
Lavington		3 10				
Edington and Bratton		3 18				
12 OXFORD 56 ...... dep.	1212	12 20	11 8	2 2	212	2 2	2 45 2 45
12 DIDCOT 56 ...... "	1211	12 33	1 37	1 37	1227	2 26	3 23 3 20
12 SWINDON .... "	1 20			2 50	3 7	5 3
Chippenham ‡ .....dep				3 20	5 22	5 37
Melksham ‡	2025			3 33	5 0 5 38	5 52
Holt ‡	2031			3 50	5 25 9	5 47 5 58
Trowbridge 48, 49 .. arr.	2038	2 50		40223 423 59	5 15	5 53 6 5
49 BRADFORD-ON-AVON arr.	3042	3 42		4 18 4 16	5 12 5 54	
49 BATH .... "	4 5 0	4 4 0		4 39 4 39	5 27 6 23	6 48 6 48
49 BRISTOL (Temple M.) "	4 25	4 25		5 15 1	5 49 6 46	7 21 7 21
48 BRISTOL (Temple M.)dep.	1012		aft	4 8	Stop	5 50 5 48
48 BATH .... "			2 54	4 37		6 14
48 BRADFORD-ON-AVON "			3 11	5 0		6 12
Trowbridge .... dep.			3 24	3 48 4 5	5 12	5 18	6 0 6 38
Westbury 48, 49 .... arr.	2 37	3 25	3 32	3251 3 56 4 13	5 25	5 26	6 8 6 46
48 SALISBURY .... arr.			4 32		6 27		7 29
Westbury .... dep.	2 42		Stop	4 2 4 16	5 30	5 55	
Frome 48 { arr.	2 20	2 51		4 11 4 27	5 41	6	6 19
{ dep.		2 54	3 13	4 13		5 45 6 7	6 40
Witham 41			Stop		5 56 6 18	6 53
Bruton ‡		m			6 7 6 27	
Castle Cary ‡		3 15 3 23			6 15 6 35	
Sparkford					6 44	
Marston Magna			aft		6 50	
Yeovil (Pen Mill) { arr.		3 29	m aft	4 45		6 58	
52 { dep.		3 32	4 54 10	4 49	5 50	7 12	
Yetminster			4 17			7 22	
Evershot			4 31			7 34	
Maiden Newton 59.. { arr.		3 53	4 40	5 11		7 40	
{ dep.		3 56	4 41	5 15		7 43	
Grimstone and Frampton			4 49			7 50	
Dorchester * ‡ 137		4 8	5 0	5 28	5 55	7 29	8 0	
Upwey Junction ‡ 54			5 12		6 7	7 32	8 9	
Weymouth (Town) ...arr.		4 20	5 20	5 40	6 15	7 40	8 15	
Keinton Mandeville		3 35				6 27	
Charlton Mackrell		3 41				6 33	
Somerton (Somerset)		3 50				6 42	
Long Sutton and Pitney		3 56				6 48	
Langport East		4 1				6 53	
Yeovil (Town) 163.. { arr.			4 12	5 52		
{ dep.			4 17	5 57		
Montacute			4 28	6 8		
Martock			4 35	6 16		
Longport West			4 47	6 27		
Athelney		4 12	4 58	6 37	7 5	
Durston 17		4 17	5 3	6 42		
Taunton 22, 54 .... arr.		4 32	4 44 5 15	6 55	7 25	
54 ILFRACOMBE 144 ... arr.			8a10 8 35			
22 EXETER (St. David's) "			5 28 6 50	8 19	8 19	
22 TORQUAY .... "			6 44 8 18	9 36	9 36	
22 PLYMOUTH (Millbay) "			7a6 1013	1013	1013	
22 PENZANCE .... "			1010			

☞ **For Steamers between Weymouth and Guernsey and Jersey, see page 912.**

"THE BUFF BOOK" (LONDON TRADES DIRECTORY) IS
IN EVERY IMPORTANT HOTEL. ASK FOR IT.

included a map. The guide survived until 1961 and, although not an official railway publication, some railways used extracts as their own timetable. At the same time Bradshaw also produced an occasional publication, *Bradshaw's Railway Manual* which contained details of every railway in the country including a summary of its routes, the names of directors and executive officers, financial details and statistics.

LONDON, READING, CHIPPENHAM, WEYMOUTH, and TAUNTON.—Great Western.

Down. — Week Days—Continued. — Sundays.

	aft	aft	aft	aft	aft	aft	aft	aft	aft	aft	aft	aft	aft	aft	aft	aft	aft	aft	mrn	mrn
PADDINGTON.........dep.	4	8	4 15			5 5			5A55	540	6 30	6A30			7 30			9 15	10 0	9 10
Reading.............. "		5 25				5 55		6 0		640	6 12	7 16			8 33			1012	11 0	1017
Reading (West)		5 29													8 36					
Theale §, for Bradfield College		5 38						6 10		650					8 45			1110		1027
Aldermaston		5 45						6 17		657					8 52			1117		1033
Midgham..................		5 51				6 10		6 23		7 3					8 58			1123		1039
Thatcham.................		5 57						6 29		7 9					9 4			1129		1045
Newbury 56 ......arr.		6 4				6 21		6 41	6 58	716		7 39			9 11			1136		1052
56 SOUTHAMPTON TOWN † arr.		Stop							8 50											
Newbury ....dep.						6 25	6 32	Stop		7 2		7 45			9 14					1055
Kintbury.................		m					6 42			7 12		7 55			9 24					11 5
Hungerford	5 55						6 48			7 20		8 2			9 30					1112
Bedwyn	6 6						el			7 30		8 12								1122
Savernake ** 59, 122, 123..	6 16					6 51	Stop			7 39		8 21			Stop					1131
Pewsey...................	6 27											8 30								1140
Woodborough..........	6 35											8 37	m							1147
Patney and Chirton.....	6 41											8 44	8 50							1153
Devizes ¶ .... { arr. dep.						m			8 1				9 0		m					12 1 / 12 3
Seend ¶.................					6 43				8 5			7g37	9 14		1030					
				6 53				8 14				9 24		1046						
Lavington	6 55					i						8 55								
Edington and Bratton	7 5											9 3								
12 OXFORD 56 ....dep.						4L30		4F55		6 2					9 40					7L40
12 DIDCOT 56 .... "						4L54		5F53		6 39					1040					8L 9
12 SWINDON .... "										7 17					1115					
Chippenham ¶.....dep.		6 15								8 30										
Melksham ¶		6 34								8 43										
Holt ¶		6 43	7 6					8 22	8 49		9 33			1058					1222
Trowbridge 48, 49.. arr.		6 51	7 17	8110				8 28	8 55		9 45			11 5		1155			
49 BRADFORD-ON-AVON arr.		7 15		8r26				9 50	9 50	9 50					Stop				1 18
49 BATH............. "		7 41		8r43				1010	1010	1010									1 38
49 BRISTOL (Temple M.) "		8 14		9r 9				1033	1033	1033									2 8
48 BRISTOL (Temple M.) dep.		6 8	6r20					7 53			8 45			1050	1050		10 0		
48 BATH.............. "		6 40						7r39			9 8			1115	1115		1029		
48 BRADFORD-ON-AVON "		6 56						8r 7			9 24			1132	1132		1052		
Trowbridge ....dep.		7 10						9 0			9 37			1145	12 0		1110		
Westbury 48, 49........arr.	7 15	7 18		7 26	aft			9 8	9 11		9 45	aft		1153	a		1118		
48 SALISBURY .... "				8 33	m						1032	m							
Westbury ....dep.				7 33	8 10						Stop		9 53		1155		1125		
Frome 48............ { arr. dep.			7 29	7 42	8 21								10 4	12 5			1135		
				7 44	8 22												1138		
Witham 41.............				aft	8 33												1149		
Bruton ‡...............				m	8 44												1158		
Castle Cary ¶				8 4	8 15	8 52											12 5		
Sparkford					9 3											1214			
Marston Magna........					9 9											1220			
Yeovil (Pen Mill) { arr.			aft	8 18	9 18										1255	1228			
52 { dep.	7 45			8 21											1259	1234			
Yetminster...........				8 31												1247			
Evershot.............				8 43												1 2			
Maiden Newton 59.. { arr. dep.				8 49 / 8 51						aft					aft	1 8 / 1 13			
Grimstone and Frampton..										m					m				
Dorchester * ¶ 137.....				9 2						9 55					1145	1 23			
Upwey Junction ¶ 54....										1010									
Weymouth (Town)....arr.				9 15						1020					12 0	2K2	1 40		
Keinton Mandeville.......					8 27														
Charlton Mackrell.......					8 33														
Somerton (Somerset)....					8 42														
Long Sutton and Pitney ..					8 48														
Langport East.........					8 53														
Yeovil (Town) 163.. { arr. dep.			7 47 / 8 0																
Montacute...........			8 12																
Martock..............			8 21																
Langport West.......			8 33																
Atheiney.............			8 45			9 4													
Durston 17..........			8 50			9 11													
Taunton 22, 54... arr.			9 5			9 25													
54 ILFRACOMBE 144.... arr.																			
22 EXETER (St. David's) "			1040			1040													
22 TORQUAY.......... "			1149			1149													
22 PLYMOUTH (Millbay) "			1235			1235													
PENZANCE .... "																			

For Notes and SUNDAY TRAINS, see page 6.

George **Bradshaw** was born in Lancashire in 1801 and after serving an apprenticeship as an engraver set up his own business as a printer of maps. In 1839, soon after the first railways were built, he published the first railway timetable. He published many other titles including *Bradshaw's Continental Guide* which helped to make foreign travel possible. In *Around the World in Eighty Days* Jules Verne made sure that Phileas Fogg had a copy in his pocket.

LONDON, READING, CHIPPENHAM, WEYMOUTH, and TAUNTON.—Great Western.

Down. — **Sundays**—*Continued.*

	aft	aft	aft	aft	aft	aft	aft	aft	aft	aft
PADDINGTON.........dep.		1230	2 40				2 0	5 20		
Reading............... "		1248					3 42	6 35		
Reading (West)										
Theale§, for Bradfield College							6 45			
Aldermaston							6 52			
Midgham							6 58			
Thatcham							7 4			
Newbury................arr.							7 11			
SOUTHAMPTON TOWN † arr.										
Newbury.............dep.							7 13			
Kintbury							7 23			
Hungerford							7 31			
Bedwyn							7 41			
Savernake ** 122,123							7 50			
Pewsey							7 59			
Woodborough							8 6			
Patney and Chirton						7 0	8 14			
Devizes ¶ {arr.							8 20			
{dep.						8g16	8 25			
Seend ¶										
Lavington						7 10				
Edington and Bratton						7 18				
15 OXFORD..........dep.		1 18			4 37					
15 DIDCOT............ "		2 0			5 35					
15 SWINDON.......... "		2 50			6 47					
Chippenham ¶ ...dep.		3 26			7 35					
Melksham ¶		3 40			7 50					
Holt ¶		3 47								
Trowbridge 48, 49...arr.		3 53	6 † 7		8 0	8 44				
49 BRADFORD-ON-AVON a.		4 29	6 22							
49 BATH.............. "		4 46	6 42							
49 BRISTOL (Temple M.) "		5 19								
48 BRISTOL (Temple M.) dep.				5 25		6 15				
48 BATH............... "				3 55		6 45				
48 BRADFORD-ON-AVON "				4 12		7 11				
Trowbridge...........dep.		4 30		4 30		8 8				
Westbury 48, 49.....arr.		4 0	8 4 27	4 38	7 25	8 16				
48 SALISBURY........arr.				5 39						
Westbury............dep.	2 2	4 32		4 45						
Frome 48 {arr.	2 13			4 55						
{dep.	2 16			4 58						
Witham 41	2 28			5 11						
Bruton ‡	2 39			5 20						
Castle Cary ¶	2 50			5 28						
Sparkford				5 37						
Marston Magna				5 43						
Yeovil (Pen Mill) {arr.				5 51						
{dep.				5 56						
Yetminster				6 6						
Evershot				6 18						
Maiden Newton 59. {arr.	m			6 24						
{dep.	3 53			6 26						
Grimstone and Frampton			m		m			m		
Dorchester * ¶ 139			5 30	6 40	7 30		9 15			
Upwey Junction ¶	4 22		5 43		7 42		9 29			
Weymouth (Town)....arr.	4 30		5 50	6 52	7 50		9 40			
Keinton Mandeville.....arr.	3 4									
Charlton Mackrell										
Somerton (Somerset)	3 19									
Long Sutton and Pitney	3 25									
Langport East	3 29									
Yeovil (Town)....... {arr.										
{dep.										
Montacute										
Martock										
Langport West										
Athelney										
Durston 21............arr.										
Taunton 25............arr.			5 29							
ILFRACOMBE.........arr.										
25 EXETER (St. David's) "			6 16							
25 TORQUAY.......... "			7 27							
25 PLYMOUTH (Millbay) "			7 55							
25 PENZANCE.......... "										

In the column between "aft" headers: Weymouth, Exeter, Torquay, and Plymouth Express. / Leaves Bridport at 3 20 aft., see page 58.

NOTES.

a North Road Station.
A Through Carriage to Southampton.
a Calls at Westbury 12 7 ngt. to set down on informing the Guard at Trowbridge.
b Motor Car, one class only.
B Except Mondays.
c Stapleton Road.
d Sets down from London at 6 45 aft. on informing Guard at Paddington.
F Via Newbury.
g Via Patney and Chirton.
h Via Radstock, see page 48.
i Via Westbury.
I Sets down from Reading and beyond at 7 14 aft. on informing Guard at Reading.
k By slip carriage.
K Weymouth (Landing Stage).
L Via Reading.
m Motor Car, one class only.
n Stapleton Rd., via Westbury, one class only.
p Via Westbury. Motor Car, one class only.
s Via Exeter and L. & S.W. Line.
* Over ½ mile to L. & S.W. Sta.
† Station for Docks.
‡ 1½ miles to Cole Station, L. & S.W. and Midland.
§ 3½ miles to Bradfield College.
•• About ¼ mile to M. & S.W. Station.
¶ "Halts" at Bromham and Rowde, between Devizes and Seend; at Semington, between Seend and Holt; at Lacock and at Beanacre, between Chippenham and Melksham; at Broughton Gifford, between Melksham and Holt; at Staverton, between Holt and Trowbridge; at Monkton and Came (Golf Links) and at Upwey Wishing Well, between Dorchester and Upwey Junction, at Radipole, between Upwey Junction and Weymouth; and at Alford, between Castle Cary and Keinton Mandeville.

☞ **For Local Trains** and **intermediate Stations**
BETWEEN .... PAGE
Paddington and Reading.. 32

** For Local Trains
BETWEEN .... PAGE
Yeovil (Pen Mill) and Yeovil (Town) 52

** For other Trains
BETWEEN .... PAGE
Paddington and Taunton 12
London and Weymouth 134
Trowbridge & Westbury 48
Dorchester & Weymouth 134
Upwey Junction & Weymouth 54, 134
Durston and Taunton 12

☞ **For Steamers between Weymouth and Guernsey and Jersey, see page 912.**

Great Western Railway.   For History and Financial Position, see "BRADSHAW'S RAILWAY MANUAL," annually, 740 pages, 25s. net.
HENRY BLACKLOCK & CO. Ltd., 5, Surrey Street, Strand, London, W.C.2.

Bradshaw joined the Society of Friends (The Quakers) and worked hard to improve the lives of the poor by starting schools and soup kitchens.
In 1853 he travelled to Norway contracted cholera and died there. He is buried at Oslo cathedral.

TAUNTON, WEYMOUTH, CHIPPENHAM, READING, and LONDON.—Great Western.

Miles from Taunton.	Up. / Week Days.	mrn	mrn	mrn	mrn	mrn	mrn	mrn	mrn	mrn	mrn	mrn	mrn	mrn	mrn	mrn	mrn	mrn	mrn	mrn	mrn
	27 Penzance...........dep.																				
	27 Plymouth (Millbay). "																				
	27 Torquay........... "																				
	27 Exeter (St. David's). "																				
	54 Ilfracombe 144 ... "																	m			
—	**Taunton**..............dep.															7 25		8 31			
5½	Durston															7 45		8 48			
8	Athelney															7 51		8 55			
13	Langport West															8 3					
18	Martock															8 18					
20½	Montacute															8 26					
25½	**Yeovil** (Town) 52, 163 arr.															8 35					
	dep.															8 40					
13	**Langport East**																	9 6			
15	**Long Sutton and Pitney**																	9 12			
17½	Somerton (Somerset)															Arrives Durston at 7 35 mrn.		9 19			
20¾	**Charlton Mackrell**																	9 29			
23	Keinton Mandeville ¶																	9 37			
—	Mls. **Weymouth** (Town) ¶ dep.																7 25			8 55	
—	2¼ Upwey Junction ¶																7 32				
—	7 **Dorchester** *																7 44			9 11	
—	11 Grimstone & Frampton																7 53	Arrives Durston at 8 43 mrn.			
—	14¾ Maiden Newton 59 arr.																8 1			9 22	
	dep.																8 5			9 24	
—	18 Evershot																8 15				
—	23¾ Yetminster																8 26				
—	27½ **Yeovil** (Pen Mill) 52 arr.															8 45	8 34			9 43	
	dep.																8 50			9 47	
—	31¾ **Marston Magna**																8 59				
—	34½ **Sparkford**																9 7				
27¾	**Castle Cary**																9 18	9 49		10 5	
31½	Bruton ‡	Except Mondays.															9 28				
36½	Witham 41																9 42		9 51		
41¾	**Frome 48** arr.				m												9 51		10 0	10 24	
	dep.				6 40						8 30			8 55			9 56		1035	10 27	
47½	**Westbury 48, 49** arr.				6 51						8 39			9 4			10 5			10 36	
—	49 Salisbury........dep.	2 50									7 30									9l35	
—	**Westbury**...........dep.			6 45	6 52			7 30			8 43	8 48		9 9			10 24			10 43	1045
51½	**Trowbridge 48, 49** ... arr.	3 39			7 1			7 38				8 55					10 32		Via Radstock, see page 48.		1052
54½	49 Bradford-on-Avon arr.				7 19			7 54				9k9									1124
64½	49 Bath............. "	4 9			7 39			8 17				9k32									1117
75½	49 Bristol (Temple M.) "	4 35			8 12			8 50				10k15			m				1150		1140
—	48 Bristol (Temple M.) dep.	Stop				6 0					7h5				8 15		9 15			9i15	
—	48 Bath............ "					6 24									8 36		9k45			9p45	
—	48 Bradford-on-Avon.. "		m			6 48				m					9 2		10k11			10p11	
—	**Trowbridge** ¶ ....dep.		6 30			7 18	7k30			8 0	8i15	9 8			9 20		10 35			10p23	
54½	Holt ¶		6 39				7k39			8 9		9 16			9 29		10 42				
57¾	Melksham ¶ ....[17, 53						7k50					9 24					10 50				
63¾	**Chippenham 12,** arr.						8k5					9 36					11 2				
80	17 Swindon.........arr.						9 5					10 23					11k57				
100¾	17 Didcot 56........ "						9 14				11J25	12J57								12J57	
110½	17 Oxford 56....... "						10 5				11J8	12 18								1J31	
51½	Edington and Bratton			6 55										9 19							
56	Lavington			7 7							b			9 33						10 56	
58½	Seend ¶		6 49							8 21					9 40						
62¾	Devizes.......... arr.		7 1	7g35		7 38				8 37			m	10g17	9 52						
	dep.		7 5			7 40				8 50			9 40		9 55						
62	Patney and Chirton		7 15	7 21						9 0	9 5		9 50	9 52	10 5						
64¾	Woodborough			7 29		7 53								9 59							
67¾	Pewsey			7 39		8 1	Breakfast Car, Chippenham to Paddington, see page 17.							10 9							
73	Savernake** 59, 122, 123			7 54		8 11					9 22			10 22							
76½	Bedwyn			8 2		8 18								10 30							
81½	Hungerford			8 11		8 28					9 34			10 41						11 30	
84½	Kintbury					8 35								10 48							
90	**Newbury 56**.......arr.					8 44					9 45			10 57						11 41	
—	56 Southampton Town dep.	mrn									7 35									9 45	
—	**Newbury**............dep.	7 55				8 47			9 10		9 49			11 1						11 44	
93½	Thatcham	8 4							9 18					11 9							
96½	Midgham	8 11				8 57			9 24					11 15							
98¾	Aldermaston	8 17							9 30					11 21							
101¾	Theale §, for Bradfield College	8 26							9 37					11 28							
106	Reading (West) 47 ......[70	8 35												11 37							
107	**Reading 32, 36, 47, 60,** arr.	8 38				9 12	9b37		9 51		10b11	11b42		11 42						12 7	
143	**PADDINGTON**........ "	9 30				10 0	1015		1045		10 52	12 20		12 55						12 55	

For Notes, see page 11; for Continuation of Trains, see pages 8 to 11.

HOTEL VICTORIA,
NEWQUAY, CORNWALL.
Only Hotel in England with Electric Lift from every floor
to Bathing Beaches.
Officially appointed Hotel to the R.A.C., A.A., & M.U.
Finest Garage in the West of England.
EXPERT REPAIRERS.   FIRST-CLASS GOLF.

Taunton, Weymouth, &c., to London.]   8   [Great Western

TAUNTON, WEYMOUTH, CHIPPENHAM, READING, and LONDON.—Great Western.

Up. — Week Days—Continued.

Station																						
	mrn	mrn	mrn	mrn	mrn	mrn	mrn	non	mrn	aft	mrn	mrn	mrn	aft	mrn	mrn	aft	aft	mrn	aft		
															10 0							
27 Penzance...........dep.				7 10		8 30				8 40				1115	12 30							
27 Plymouth (Millbay). "				7 0		9 1				9 23				1210				11 0				
27 Torquay............ "				8 58		10 15				1033					1 45							
27 Exeter (St. David's). "						8 X 0								10 2 5								
54 Ilfracombe 144..... "																	12 30					
Taunton............dep.				10 0		11 0				1125							1232	1245				
Durston................				1015						1140	1156							1252				
Athelney...............				1021						1146	12 3						Stop	1 3				
Langport West.........				1036						1157								1 17				
Martock...............				1047						12 9								1 25				
Montacute.............				1053						1215								1 37				
Yeovil (Town) 52, 163 { arr.				11 2						1224								1 37				
{ dep.				11 4						1228								1 40				
Langport East.........										1214												
Long Sutton and Pitney										1220												
Somerton (Somerset)...										1226												
Charlton Mackrell.....										1234												
Keinton Mandeville ¶..	mrn								mrn	1240			mrn				mrn				
Weymouth (Town) ..dep.	9 30					10 30		1122			1150					1 0					
Upwey Junction ¶......	9 38							1130								1 8					
Dorchester⁵............	9 54					10 47		1144			12 7					1 24					
Grimstone and Frampton..	10 4							Stop								1 34					
Maiden Newton 59.... { arr.	10 12					10 58					1218					1 42					
{ dep.	10 13					11 3					1222					1 44					
Evershot..............	10 23										1232					1 54					
Yetminster...........	10 33										1241					2 4					
Yeovil (Pen Mill)... { arr.	10 44		11 8			11 21				1230	1249					2 15		1 42			
52 { dep.	Stop		Stop			11 25	12 0				1254					Stop		Stop			
Marston Magna........							12 9											Stop			
Sparkford............							1216														
Castle Cary..........							1226		1252	1 11											
Bruton ¶.............							1234		mrn				1 41								
Witham 41............							1246	1255					1 50								
Frome 48.......... { arr.						12 0	1255	1 6		1 30											
{ dep.						12 3	1258	1 9		1 34			Stop								
Westbury 48, 49..... arr.					Slip	12 12	1 7	1 18		1 43											
49 Salisbury.......dep.				mrn		10 48			1235	1235	mrn					aft					
Westbury........... dep.				1158		12 18		1 20	1 35	1 49	1 53					2 12					
Trowbridge 48, 49... arr.						12 25		1 28	1 42		2 1					2 19					
49 Bradford-on-Avon. arr.						12 54			1 58							2235					
49 Bath............. "						1 17			2 17							2258					
49 Bristol (Temple M.) "						1 47			2 54							3 33	aft				
48 Bristol (Temple M.)dep.	1010	10 10				1125				1 5						1 52	22				
48 Bath.............. "	1032	10 32				1146				1 26						1 26	2 54				
48 Bradford-on-Avon.. "	1058	10 58				12 3				1 52						1 52	5 11				
Trowbridge ¶........dep.	1112	11 30				12 29				1 24	2 10					2 30	2 25				
Holt ¶...............	1122	11 37				1215	12 37				2 17					2 38	2 32				
Melksham ¶...17, 53	1131					12 45										2 50					
Chippenham 12... arr.	1150					12 57										3 2					
17 Swindon........ arr.	1256					1 23										3 48					
17 Didcot 56........ "	2 55					2 58				3 32						4 48					
17 Oxford 56........ "	2 15					2 15				5 21						5 21					
Edington and Bratton......				19 8												3 42					
Lavington............				1219												3 42					
Seend ¶..............			11 48			1229				2 27						3 52					
Devizes........... { arr.			11 58	1g16		1233				2 39						3 57					
{ dep.			12 3							2 43											
Patney and Chirton......			12 12	1231		1244				2 53						4 6					
Woodborough.........			12 18													4 12					
Pewsey..............			12 26													4 20					
Savernake ** 59, 122, 123 ..			12 37													4 31					
Bedwyn.............			12 45			1 6									aft	4 38					
Hungerford..........			12 54			1 15		1 43							3 50	4 49					
Kintbury...........						1 20		1 50							3 57	4 56					
Newbury 56........ arr.						1 26		1 59							4 6	5 5					
56 Southampton Town dep.	non		aft			1122									aft	1 50					
Newbury...........dep.	12 0		1 0			1 32		2 2							3 12½	5 9					
Thatcham............	12 8		1 8					2 9							3 20½	5 17					
Midgham............	12 14		1 14					2 16							3 26½	5 23					
Aldermaston........	12 20		1 20					2 23							3 32½	5 29					
Theale §, for Bradfield College	12 27		1 27					2 29							3 39½	5 36					
Reading (West) 47...60, 70	12 36		1 36					2 38							3 48	5 45					
Reading 32, 36 47...arr.	12 40	2 30	1 39		1255	1 50	2 30	2 41		2 58				3 55	4 45	5 28½	506	165 48			
Paddington........ "	1 50	2 40		2 30		1 30	2 50	3 45													

☞ For Steamers between Jersey, Guernsey, and Weymouth, see page 912.

MANDEVILLE HOTEL,

Mandeville Place, Wigmore St., Cavendish Sq.

HIGH-CLASS well-appointed Private Hotel. Spacious Drawing, Dining Rooms, and Lounge. Electric Light. Within easy access of Shops and Theatres. First-class Cuisine. Self-contained Suites.

Under Personal Supervision of Proprietress.
TERMS ON APPLICATION.

Tel.: Townsfolk, London.   Tel.: Pad. 153.

THE GRANTLEIGH,

12-18, INVERNESS TERRACE, HYDE PARK, W.2.

Healthy position, close to Queen's Road Tube, Metropolitan Station, and Buses. Absolutely quiet.

Under entirely New Management.

Tel.: Park 794.   **RESIDENT PROPRIETRESS.**

TAUNTON, WEYMOUTH, CHIPPENHAM, READING, and LONDON.—Great Western.

Up. — Week Days—*Continued.*

	aft	mrn	aft	aft	aft	aft	aft	aft	aft	mrn	mrn	aft	aft	aft		aft	mrn	aft	aft	aft
27 PENZANCE..........dep.										10 0	11 0					...	10 0			
27 PLYMOUTH (Millbay). "		10 25								1 0	2 0					...	1 0			
27 TORQUAY .... "		10 55									1249	2 23					...| 1249			
27 EXETER (St. David's) "		12 20								2 26	3 27					...	2 26			
54 ILFRACOMBE 144... "		9 30								12₅5	12₅5					...	12₅5			
Taunton..........dep.		1 50	1 35							3 25	4 12					...	4 0			
Durston............										3 39						...	4 25			
Athelney............			1 54							3 46						...	4 32			
Langport West......										m						...	4 50			
Martock............																	5 4			
Montacute..........																	5 11			
Yeovil (Town) 52, {arr. 163 {dep.																	5 22			
																	5 25			
Langport East......			2 5							3 57										
Long Sutton and Pitney			2 10							4 2										
Somerton (Somerset)..			2 16			m				4 8										
Charlton Mackrell....			2 24			2 30				4 16										
Keinton Mandeville ¶		m				m	2 40			4 22									m
Weymouth (Town)¶..dep.	1 30				2 50				3 10			3 25		4 18					5 28
Upwey Junction ¶......	1 38				2 58							3 32							5 35
Dorchester*..........	1 52				3 12				3 26			3 45		4 32					5 50
Grimstone and Frampton..												3 54							Stop
Maiden Newton 59.. {arr. {dep.									3 37			4 2		4 43					
									3 41			4 7		4 46					
Evershot...........												4 18							
Yetminster.........												4 31							
Yeovil (Pen Mill) {arr. 52 {dep.							m		4 0			4 39		5 5	5 27			
							2 50		4 4			Stop		5 9					
Marston Magna......							3 0												
Sparkford..........							3 8						m						
Castle Cary........						3 0	3 20			4 32			4 50						
Bruton ‡...........							3 29					aft	4 59						
Witham 41.........							3 42					4 58	5 12						
Frome 48.......... {arr. {dep.		2 25					3 53	4 39				5 7	5 23						
		2 28					3 54	4 42											
Westbury 48, 49.....arr.		2 38				4 6	4 51		5 6										
49 SALISBURY..........dep.					2 35			m		4 24			4 24						
Westbury............dep.		2 42	3 19			4 10	4 12 4 57		5 10 5 20			5 25		4 50					aft
Trowbridge 48, 49...arr.		2 50	3 27			4 22 5 4						5 32		m 6 4					6 15
49 BRADFORD-ON-AVON arr.			3 42			5 20						5 54							6 22
49 BATH............. "			4 0			5 37						6 23		aft					7₅15
49 BRISTOL(Temple M.). "			4₅25			5 59						6 46		m					6 48
48 BRISTOL(Temple M.).dep.					2 22							Stop		3 30					7 21
48 BATH............. "					2 54									4₅37	4 20				Stop
48 BRADFORD-ON-AVON. "					3 11									5 10	4 46	m			
Trowbridge ¶........dep.					3₅50		4 35		4 ₅5					5₅18		3 30			
Holt ¶..............					3₅58		4 43									5 56	6 18	m		
Melksham ¶....17, 53 Chippenham 12, arr.					4 8		4 49									5 14		6 45	
					4₅25											5 29		6 0	
17 SWINDON ....arr.																6 42		6 42	
17 DIDCOT 56......... "														7₅55		8 20		8 20	
17 OXFORD 56 .... "														8₅28		9 15		9 15	
Edington and Bratton.....						4 19													Stop
Lavington..........						4 29											6 27		
Seend ¶............																	6 38		
Devizes .... {arr. {dep.						5₅25													
Patney and Chirton......						4 42													
Woodborough........						4 48													
Pewsey............						4 56													
Savernake** 59, 122, 123...						5 9					6 15								
Bedwyn.............						5 18					6 22							aft
Hungerford.....".....						5 28					6 32							7 10
Kintbury...........											6 39							7 17
Newbury 56..........											6 45							7 26
56 SOUTHAMPTON TOWN dep.														4 50				4 50
Newbury............dep.														7 0				7 31
Thatcham..........																		7 39
Midgham...........																		7 46
Aldermaston........																		7 52
Theale §, for Bradfield College																		8 5
Reading (West) 47..{60,70																		8 8
Reading 32,36, 47....arr.									7₅23					7 23	7 57			8 16
PADDINGTON........ "									6 50					8 10	8 45			9 20

For Notes, see page 11; for Continuation of Trains, see pages 10 and 11.

LINKS HOTEL
(FULLY LICENSED),
ST. MARYCHURCH, TORQUAY.

This Ideal Golfers' Hotel is situated two minutes from TORQUAY and SOUTH DEVON (18-HOLE)
GOLF COURSE, and three minutes from the famous BABBACOMBE DOWNS.

ENLARGED, RECONSTRUCTED, AND THOROUGHLY BROUGHT UP TO DATE.

Excellent New Lounge.　　Billiard and Ball Room.　　New Garage.
Hot and Cold Water in all Bedrooms.　　Electric Light.　　Central Heating.
ALL-WEATHER TENNIS COURT, CHAMPIONSHIP SIZE.

Inclusive Terms from 5 Guineas per week.

Telephone: **913** TORQUAY.　　　　Particulars on application to Proprietor, **JAMES A. PENNY.**

Taunton, Weymouth, &c., to London.]　　10　　[Great Western

TAUNTON, WEYMOUTH, CHIPPENHAM, READING, and LONDON.—Great Western.

Up.	Week Days—Continued.	Sundays.

(Detailed timetable columns — times for Week Days continued and Sundays)

Station	mrn	aft	aft	aft	aft	aft	aft	aft	aft	aft	aft	aft	noon	aft	aft	aft	mrn	mrn	mrn	noon
27 PENZANCE ....dep.	11 0												12 0							
27 PLYMOUTH (Millbay) "	2 a0												4a10	4 20						
27 TORQUAY "	2 23												4 24	5 22						
27 EXETER (St. David's) "	3 27					3 43							5 50	7 10						
54 ILFRACOMBE 144 "						1 55							3 z 0	4 25						
Taunton ....dep.	4 45					6 55							7 50	9 0						
Durston "	m					6 9							8 5	9 20						
Athelney "	5 2					6 15							8 11	9 26						
Langport West						6 28								9 36						
Martock						6 40								9 46						
Montacute						6 48							m	9 52						
Yeovil(Town)52,163 {arr.						6 57								10 1						
{dep.						7 3								10 6						
Langport East	5 16												8 22							
Long Sutton and Pitney	5 22												8 27							
Somerton (Somerset)	5 30												8 33							
Charlton Mackrell	5 39												8 41							
Keinton Mandeville ¶	5 47							m					8 47							
Weymouth (Town) ¶ ..dep.							6 0	6 50	7 25					9 10	11 0	m			9 0	
Upwey Junction ¶							6 7	6 58						9 18	11 9				9 18	
Dorchester*							6 23	7 12	7 41					9 35	1122					
Grimstone and Frampton							6 32		7 49											
Maiden Newton 59.. {arr.							6 40		7 57										9 29	
{dep.							6 50		8 0										9 39	
Evershot							7 1		8 10										9 43	
Yetminster							7 10		8 19										9 55	
Yeovil (Pen Mill) {arr.						7 5	7 18		8 27				10 8						10 3	
52 {dep.					5 42	Stop	7 28		8 32				Stop						1013	
Marston Magna					5 51		7 37												1024	
Sparkford					6 4		7 53												1034	
Castle Cary	5 58				6 19		8 11		8 48				9 0						1050	
Bruton ‡					6 31		8 20						9 8						11 0	
Witham 41					6 44		7 46	8 33					9 20						1116	
Frome 48 {arr.		m			6 53		7 55	8 42		9 8			9 31						1125	
{dep.		6 33			7 2		8 5	8 49		9 10			9 34						1136	12 0
Westbury 48, 49 arr.		6 44			7 11			8 58		9 19			9 35						1145	
49 SALISBURY ....dep.						7 20			7 50								2 50			
Westbury ....dep.	6 30	6 55					8 3			9 29									1151	
Trowbridge 48, 49 "	6 37						8 10			9 36							3 39		1158	
49 BRADFORD-ON-AVON. arr.	7x15						8 26			9 50						4 9			1 15	
49 BATH "	7z41						8 43 aft			1010						4 35			1 35	
49 BRISTOL (Temple M.) "	8z14			m		9 c 9	m	9z15		1033	m								2 8	1 22
48 BRISTOL (Temple M.)dep.	5z50		5z50		6 8		7 3				8 45								10 6	
48 BATH "	6 14		6 14		6 40		7 39				9 8								1029	
48 BRADFORD-ON-AVON "	6 12		6 12		6 56		8 7				9 24		aft						1052	
Trowbridge ¶ ......dep.	6 50		6 58		7 28		8 25				9 50		10 0				7 5		12 3	
Holt ¶	6 55		7 5		7 38		8 33				9 58									
Melksham ¶ ...[17,53	7 7				7 46		8 42						1013						1221	
Chippenham 12, "	7 19				8 5		8 59						1027						1233	
17 SWINDON ....arr.					8 43		10k0						1058						1 7	
17 DIDCOT 56 .... "													1 7				10y32	2 15		
17 OXFORD 56 .... "					9 47								7z15				11 J 5	3 32		
Edington and Bratton			7 8																	
Lavington "			7 22																	
Seend				7 18							10 8						7 26			
Devizes .... {arr.		9 y 0		7 28							1020						7 30			
{dep.				7 37													7 41			
Patney and Chirton			7 35	7 50													7 49			
Woodborough			Stop	7 59													8 0			
Pewsey "				8 10													8 12			
Savernake ** 59, 122, 123.				8 24													8 21			
Bedwyn				8 33			aft										8 32			
Hungerford				8 44			9 55										8 39			
Kintbury				8 51			10 1										8 45			
Newbury 56 ....arr.				9 0			1010													
55 SOUTHAMPTON TOWN.dep.		aft					7z25													
Newbury ....dep.		8 20	9 3				1012										8 51			
Thatcham "		8 28	9 11				1020										9 0			
Midgham "		8 34	9 17				1026										9 8			
Aldermaston "		8 40	9 23														9 16			
Theale§, for Bradfield College		8 47	9 30				U1033										9 23			
Reading(West) 47.. [60,70																				
Reading 32, 36, 47.. "		8 57	9 42		9 35		1045							1 47				9 33	2 42	
PADDINGTON "		1025	10 45		1025									2 45				10 50	3 35	

☞ **For Steamers between Jersey, Guernsey, and Weymouth, see page 912.**

Main Line.]   **11**   **[Great Western.**

TAUNTON, WEYMOUTH, CHIPPENHAM, READING, and LONDON.—Great Western.

Up. — Sundays—*Continued.*

	aft	aft	aft	aft	mrn	aft	aft	aft	aft	aft	aft	NOTES.
30 PENZANCE ....dep.					11 10							
30 PLYMOUTH (Millbay) .. "					2630							*a* North Road Station.
30 TORQUAY .... "					3 0							*b* Slip Carriage.
30 EXETER (St. David's) .. "					4 5							**b** Calls at Lavington at 8 53 mrn. to pick up for Reading
ILFRACOMBE .... "												and beyond on notice being
Taunton ....dep.					4 50							given at the Station not later than 8 30 mrn.
Durston												*c* Stapleton Road.
Atheiney												*d* Calls at Lavington to pick up
Langport West												for Reading and beyond on
Martock												notice being given at the Station not later than 5 55 aft.
Montacute.............												F Via Newbury.
Yeovil (Town) { arr.		**m**										*g* Via Patney and Chirton.
.... { dep.												*h* Via Radstock, see page 48.
Langport East		3 53										**h** Passengers may secure Sleeping Car accommodation be-
Long Sutton and Pitney ..		3 59										tween York and Aberdeen
Somerton (Somerset)......		4 5										(Saturday nights excepted)
Charlton Mackrell												by notifying any Station
Keinton Mandeville ¶ ...		**m**	22			**m**		**m** **m**				Master en route before 3 aft. on the day required.
Weymouth (Town) ¶ ..dep.	2 0		3 25			4 50		6 45 8 45				*i* Via Westbury.
Upwey Junction ¶.......	2 8					4 58		6 53 8 53				*j* Via Reading.
Dorchester *...........	2 23		3 44			5 12		7 7 9 10				*k* Motor Car, one class only.
Grimstone and Frampton..								Stop Stop				L L. & S. W. Station.
Maiden Newton 59. { arr.	2 43		3 55									**m** Motor Car, one class only.
.... { dep.			4 14									*p* Via Westbury. Motor Car, one class only.
Evershot..............			4 14									*s* Saturdays only.
Yetminster............			4 27									*t* Except Sunday mornings.
Yeovil (Pen Mill)....{ arr.			4 35									U Wednesdays only.
.... { dep.	3 0		4 40									X Passengers find their own
Marston Magna	3 9											way between Barnstaple
Sparkford	3 21						aft.					Junction (L. & S. W.) and Barnstaple (G. W.).
Castle Cary	3 37	4 32 5 1					5435					*z* Via L. & S.W. Line and Exeter.
Bruton ‡..............	3 48						5446					
Witham 41............	4 18						6 x 5 aft					* Over ¼ mile to L. & S. W.
Frome 48............{ arr.	4 22	5 21					6x15 m					Station.
...........{ dep.	4 34	5 24					6 456 55					‡ 1¼ mile to Cole Station,
Westbury 48, 49...arr.	4 43	5 33 5 47					7 6					L. & S. W. and Midland.
49 SALISBURY.........dep.	12 L 0											§ 3¼ miles to Bradfield College.
Westbury ....dep.	4 55	5 54			6 0	7 10 8 30						About ¼ mile to M. & S. W. Station.
Trowbridge 48, 49...arr.					6 7	7 19 8 37						¶ "Halts" at Alford, between
49 BRADFORD-ON-AVON.. arr.					6 22							Keinton Mandeville and Castle
49 BATH .... "					6 42							Cary; at Radipole, between
49 BRISTOL (Temple Md.) "					7 48 7							Weymouth and Upwey Junc-
48 BATH .... "	3 25	3 25	3 25									tion; at Upwey Wishing Well
48 BATH .... "	3 55	3 55	3 55									and at Monkton and Came
48 BRADFORD-ON-AVON.. "	4 12	4 12	4 12									Golf Links, between Upwey
Trowbridge ¶.........dep.	4 30	4 30	5 35	6 20								Junction and Dorchester; at
Holt ¶...............			5 44									Staverton, between Trow-
Melksham ¶ ....{ 21, 53	21, 53		6 36									bridge and Holt; at Broughton Gifford, between Holt and
Chippenham 15, arr.			6 48									Melksham; at Beanacre and
21 SWINDON ....arr.			7 29									at Lacock, between Melk-
21 DIDCOT .... "			8 40									sham and Chippenham; at
21 OXFORD .... "			9 47									Semington, between Holt and Seend; and at Bromham and
Edington and Bratton	5 13											Rowde, between Seend and
Lavington	5 31											Devizes.
Seend ¶			5 56									
Devizes ....{ arr.	8y22		6 6									
..........{ dep.			6 16									
Patney and Chirton	5 41		6 28									**For other Trains**
Woodborough..........			6 34									BETWEEN PAGE
Pewsey			6 43									Taunton and Durston 17
Savernake** 122, 123..			6 55									Taunton and Paddington 17
Bedwyn..............			7 3									Weymouth and Upwey
Hungerford...........			7 14									Junction.............54, 137
Kintbury			7 21									Weymouth & Dorchester 137
Newbury ....arr.			7 30									Weymouth and London .. 137
SOUTHAMPTON TOWN ..												Westbury and Trowbridge 49
Newbury ....dep.			7 35									
Thatcham			7 44									
Midgham............			7 50									
Aldermaston.........			7 56									
Theale §, for Bradfield College			8 4									
Reading (West) 47...{70												
Reading 34, 38, 47, 64, arr.		9 15	8 14	9 5								
PADDINGTON .... "		7 45	9 15	9 55								

For **LOCAL TRAINS** between Yeovil (Town) and Yeovil (Pen Mill), see page 52.
For **LOCAL TRAINS** and intermediate Stations between Reading and Paddington, see page 36.

LONDON, READING, TAUNTON, EXETER, PLYMOUTH, and PENZANCE.—Great Western.

Miles from Paddington.	Down.	Week Days.																		
		aft	mrn	mrn	mrn	mrn	mrn	mrn	mn	mrn	ngt.	mrn	mrn	mrn	mrn	mrn	mrn	mrn	mrn	mrn
	12 PADDINGTON.....dep.	10 0									12 0									
	12 READING .... "	10 48									1250									
	12 OXFORD .... "	10J40																8c48		
	12 BATH .... "	12J40									2 57							4c17		
	12 BRISTOL (Temp. Mds.) "	1 8									3 30							6 20		
		mrn	mrn	mrn	mrn	mrn	mrn	mrn	mn	mrn	mrn	mrn	mrn	mrn	mrn	mrn	mrn	mrn	mrn	mrn
—	Taunton ....dep.	2 8									4 36						7 5	7 49		
145	Norton Fitzwarren........																7 10			
150	Wellington																7 23			
154¼	Burlescombe........																7 34			
158¾	Tiverton Junction 50, 118..	Sleeping Car (1st Class).									Except Mondays.						7 46	8 20		
161	Cullompton																7 56			
165¼	Hele and Bradninch																8 5			
166¾	Silverton																8 9			
170¼	Stoke Canon 51																8 19			
173¾	Exeter (St. David's) * 40, 51, 141, 142, 144 arr.	2 46									5 15						8 25	8 38		
	Exeter (St. David's) dep	2 55									5 24				6 45	8 5		8 45		9 0
174¼	Exeter (St. Thomas) 40														6 55	8 9				9 6
178¼	Exminster........														7 3	8 17				
182¼	Starcross †														7 14	8 25				
184¼	Dawlish Warren........														7 19	8 30				
185¾	Dawlish														7 25	8 35				9 27
188¾	Teignmouth, for Bishop's [Teignton										5 52				7 35	8 44				9 36
193¾	Newton Abbot § 51 ....arr.	n 3 23									6 1				7 44	8 53				9 45
206	51 MORETONHAMPSTEAD arr.														8 37					1041
199¾	51 TORQUAY........ "	4t10									7 12				8 14	9 19				10 6
201¾	51 PAIGNTON .... "	7 22									7 22				8 26	9 31				1018
208¾	51 KINGSWEAR........ "	7 44									7 44				8 47	9 53				1042
—	Newton Abbot........dep.	3 32									6 11			7 30	8 5	Stop				10 0
202¼	Totnes 57........										6 32			7 49	8 25					1019
209¼	Brent 54													8 9	8 44					1042
222	54 KINGSBRIDGE ......arr.													9 5						1140
211½	Wrangaton........		Third Class only.											8 16	8 50					1048
212¾	Bittaford Platform													8 20	8 54					1052
215	Ivybridge........													8 25	8 59					1057
217½	Cornwood													8 31	9 5					11 3
221¾	Plympton........													8 39	9 13					1111
225¼	Plymouth 52, 142 (Mutley)........													8 45	9 19					1117
225¾	Plymouth (North Road)........	4 25									7 11			8 48	9 22	m		10 0		1120
226½	Plymouth (Millbay)..arr.	4 55									7 20			8 56	9 30	mrn		10 22	m	1130
—	Plymouth (Millbay)....dep.		5 40			6 8						7N30		9 20		9 35		9N55	1035	Stop
—	" (North Road)........	4 35							720			7 45						10 12		
227	Devonport †		5 48			6 13			728			7 51		9 28		9 40		10 20	1040	
227¾	Keyham		5 55			6 16			732			7 56		9 32		9 46			1046	
228¾	St. Budeaux Platform		5 58			6 19			736					9 36		9 49			1049	
230	Saltash, for Callington		6 2			6 24			739			8 3		9 41		9 52			1052	
230¾	Defiance Platform								743		Sleeping Car (1st Class).			9 44						
235	St. Germans........					6 35			753			8 13		9 52						
240½	Menheniot........					6 46			8 6			8 25		10 3						
243¼	Liskeard 39........	5 9				6 53			813			8 34		1012				10 50		
252¼	39 LOOE ....arr.	5 57				8 7						9 55						11 40		
246¾	Doublebois........											8 43		1021						
252½	Bodmin Road 47	5‡24										8 56		1033				11 8		
256	Lostwithiel 50							8 25				9 5		1040				11 15		
260¼	Par 50........	5 40						8 37				9 18		1053				11 27		
264¾	50 FOWEY ....arr.	6 52										9A25						11A40		
281	50 NEWQUAY .... "	7 23										1028						12 46		
265	St. Austell........	5 55						8 49				9 31		11 5				11 40		
267½	Burngullow........							8 55				9 38		1111						
271¾	Grampound Road........							9 4				9 49		1120						
274½	Probus and Ladock Platform							9 10				9 56		1125						
279¾	Truro 116........arr.	6 18						9 19				10 5		1135				12 3		aft
291	116 FALMOUTH ....arr.	7 23		m				10 2		m		11 4	m					12 57		m
—	Truro........dep.	6 26		7 40	8 0		8 35			9 55		1011	1112					12 8		1235
284½	Chacewater 50			7 53	8 12		8 48			1015		1023	1125					12 21		1248
286¾	Scorrier				8 18		8 54					1028	1132							
288¾	Redruth........	6 47			8 25		9 0					1036	1137					12 32		
290½	Carn Brea........				8 30		9 7					1042	1143							
292	Camborne........	6 58		To Newquay.	8 36		9 14			To Newquay.		1049	1150					12 42		To Newquay.
294¾	Gwinear Road 39	7 7			8 43							1057	1158					12 50		
303¾	39 HELSTON........arr.	7 35			9 15							1137						1 26		
298	Hayle........	7 15			8 52							11 5	12 6					12 58		
299½	St. Erth 39	7 23			9 0							1116	1217					1 4		
304	39 ST. IVES........arr.	7 44			9 20							1140	1237					1 25		
308¾	Marazion........	h			9 10							1127	1226					1 15		
305¾	Penzance **........arr.	7 40			9 15							1132	1232					1 20		

Through Restaurant and Sleeping Car Express (see note h), from Aberdeen and Glasgow (except on Sunday mornings) to Penzance, via Edinboro', Sheffield, Leicester, Swindon, and Plymouth, see pages 784, 791, 778, 735, 732, 669, 698, 83, and 15.

Through Carriages, Aberdeen to Plymouth and Glasgow to Exeter, via Carlisle, Crewe, and Hereford, see pages 832, 420, 450, and 12.

GREAT WESTERN HOTEL.

FIRST-CLASS RESIDENTIAL AND COUNTY.

Private Suites. Electric Light. Baths (Hot and Cold). Facing Stations. Garage opposite.
Four Packs of Hounds within easy reach. Golf. River Thames.

Telephone: 785.   Tariff from Manager.

Main Line.]   23   [Great Western.

LONDON, READING, TAUNTON, EXETER, PLYMOUTH, and PENZANCE.—Great Western.

Week Days—*Continued.*

Down.

	mrn	mrn	mrn	mrn	aft	aft	mrn	mrn	aft	aft	mrn	mrn	aft	mrn	mrn	aft	aft	aft	aft
12 PADDINGTON ....dep.				5 30								7 30			1030				
12 READING .... "				6 18								8 20							
12 OXFORD .... "												7 10							
12 BATH .... "		6 15		8 10								10 10							
12 BRISTOL Temp. Mds. "		6 50		8 40								10 50							
	mrn	mrn	mrn	mrn	aft	aft	mrn	mrn	aft	aft	mrn	mrn	aft	mrn	aft	aft	aft	aft	aft
Taunton ....dep.		9 5		10 0			1015	1015				11 50		1155					
Norton Fitzwarren		9 10					1020	1020						12 0					
Wellington		9 21					1029	1030						1211					
Burlescombe		9 31						1039						1221					
Tiverton Junction 50, 118..		9 43												1232					
Cullompton		9 51												1238					
Hele and Bradninch		10 0												1247					
Silverton		10 4												1251					
Stoke Canon 51		1013												1 0					
Exeter (St. David's) * { arr.	111	1019		10 37							111	12 27	1 6	1V30					
40, 51, 1 & 1, 142, 144 {dep.	9 30			10 45			1110		1155	12 35					1 44				
Exeter (St. Thomas) 40....	9 36						1116		12 0										
Exminster	9 44						1124		12 8										
Starcross†	9 52						1133		1216	1244									
Dawlish Warren	9 58						1138		1229										
Dawlish.......Teignton	10 5						1143		1227	1255					2 3				
Teignmouth, for Bishop's	1016						1152		1235	1 4					2 11				
Newton Abbot § 51.....arr.	1028			11 11					12 1		1 13				2 20				
51 MORETONHAMPSTEAD arr.	1058			11 44					1 22										
51 TORQUAY .... "	11 5			11 55					1227		1 47				2 46				
51 PAIGNTON .... "	11 5			12 0					1241		1 58				2 53				
51 KINGSWEAR .... "	Stop			12 16					1 3		2 19								
Newton Abbot ....dep.				11 18					1216		1 20				2 30				
Totnes 57									1236		1 38				2 48				
Brent 54				11 50					1258						3 9				
54 KINGSBRIDGE ......arr.				1 0											3 55				
Wrangaton									1 4						3 16				
Bittaford Platform......									1 8						3 20				
Ivybridge									1 14						3 25				
Cornwood									1 19						3 31				
Plympton		111							1 29						3 42				
Plymouth (Mutley)....		1152							1 35						3 48				
52, 142 (North Road)..		1153	12 16						1 38		2 15		111		4 0				
																			111
Plymouth (Millbay)....dep.			12 10	1 5			1 22		2 10		2 45				Stop				4 17
" (North Road)..		1154	12 25								2 50						2 2		
Devonport‡		1158	12 30	1 10			1 28		2 15		2 56						3 34	4 22
Keyham		12 2		1 16			1 33		2 21								3 7	4 27
St. Budeaux Platform		12 5		1 19			1 35		2 24		2 58							4 30
Saltash, for Callington		12 9	12 39	1 25			1 40		2 27		3 2						3 13	4 34
Defiance Platform		1212		1 27			1 43												
St. Germans		1220	12 48				1 51									3 23		
Menheniot		1230		Stop			2 3									3 35		
Liskeard 39			1 7				2 11									3 44		
39 LOOE ....arr.			2 10													5 25		
Doublebois							2 19									3 53		
Bodmin Road 47..........			1 23				2 32									4 6		
Lostwithiel 50..........			1 30				2 39									4 13		
Par 50			1 43				2 52									4 26		
50 FOWEY ....arr.							3 45									4A35		
50 NEWQUAY .... "			3 28													5 23		
St. Austell			1 55				3 5									4 44		
Burngullow							3 12									4 44		
Grampound Road			2 6				3 21									4 53		
Probus and Ladock Platform							3 27									4 59		
Truro 116 ....arr.			2 18	aft			3 36								4 4	5 8		
116 FALMOUTH ......arr.			3 6	111											4 52	6 7		
Truro ....dep.			2 223	0 3 15											4 9 24 254 355 14		
Chacewater 50			2 353	123 27											4 384 485 27		
Scorrier.......... aft			2 413 18												4 44 5 34		
Redruth	1 45		2 483 24												4 51 5 41		
Carn Brea..........	1 50		2 533 30												4 56 5 47		
Camborne..........	1 56		2 593 36												5 2 5 53		
Gwinear Road 39	2 2		3 63 44												4 365 8 6 0		
39 HELSTON ....arr.	3 4														5 20 6 35		
Hayle	2 10		3 133 55												5 16 6 8		
St. Erth 39	2 15		3 133 58												4 495 21 6 13		
39 ST. IVES........arr.	2 43		3 45												6 10 6 50		
Marazion	2 25		3 59												5 30 6 23		
Penzance ** ....arr.	3 30		3 35												5 6 35 6 28		

London, &c., to Penzance.]   24   [Great Western

LONDON, READING, TAUNTON, EXETER, PLYMOUTH, and PENZANCE.—Great Western.

Down. — Week Days—Continued.

	mrn	aft	aft	non	aft	aft	aft	aft	aft	aft	aft	aft	aft	mrn	mrn	aft	aft	aft	aft
12 PADDINGTON ....dep.				12 0										11 15				2 0	
12 READING	9 50														1138			2 49	
12 OXFORD	9 35														1212			1 8	
12 BATH	1144												12 32		2 13				
12 BRISTOL (Temp. Mds.)	1245												1 45		2 53				
	aft	aft	aft		aft		aft	aft	aft	aft	aft	aft	aft		aft	aft	aft	aft	aft
Taunton ....dep.	42				2 42								3 0		3 53			4 51	
Norton Fitzwarren													3 5						
Wellington													3 17						
Burlescombe													3 27						
Tiverton Junction 50, 118													3 38						
Cullompton													3 47						
Hele and Bradninch													3 57						
Silverton													4 2						
Stoke Canon 51													4 12						
Exeter (St. David's) * { arr.	2 19		3 0		3 19								4 18		4 30			5 28	
40, 51, 141, 142, 144 { dep.	2 20		383		3 29					3 40					4 37			5 33	
Exeter (St. Thomas) 40			2 43							3 45									
Exminster			2 51							3 53									
Starcross †			2 59								4 2								
Dawlish Warren			3 4							3 50	4 12								
Dawlish ....[Teignton										3 55	4 5								
Teignmouth, for Bishop's										4 5	4 21								
Newton Abbot § 51 ......arr.	2 33				3 55					4 17	4 30								
51 MORETONHAMPSTEAD arr.	3 47																		
51 TORQUAY	3 15		3 40		4 25					4 57									
51 PAIGNTON	3 25		3 57		4 36					5 12									
51 KINGSWEAR	4 19		4 19							5 33									
Newton Abbot ......dep.	3 7				4			4 15										6 18	
Totnes 57	3 25							4 34											
Brent 54	3 44							4 52											
54 KINGSBRIDGE ......arr.								6 35											
Wrangaton								4 58											
Bittaford Platform								5 2											
Ivybridge								5 7											
Cornwood								5 12											
Plympton								5 19											
Plymouth (Mutley)								5 25									7 6		
52, 142 (North Road)	4 10				4 48			5 28							6 17		7 18		
" (Millbay)..arr.	4 19							5 34							6 25				
Plymouth (Millbay) ....dep.	4 38				4 55	5 0		5 40							6 35			7 25	
" (North Road)						5 1											7 15		
Devonport †			4 47				5 7	5 47							6 40		7 22	7 30	
Keyham			4 52				5 14	5 51							6 47			7 36	
St. Budeaux Platform			4 54				5 17								6 51			7 40	
Saltash, for Callington			5 0				5 20	5 58							6 55			7 44	
Defiance Platform			5 2				5 26								6 58				
St. Germans							5 32										7 37		
Menheniot								6 7											
Liskeard 39						5 32		6 19									7 56		
39 LOOE ......arr.								6 29									8 35		
Doublebois								7 5											
Bodmin Road 47						5 49		6 37									8 13		
Lostwithiel 50						5 57		6 48									8 21		
Par 50						6 11		6 55									8 33		
50 FOWEY ......arr.						6 45		7 7									8 40		
50 NEWQUAY "						7 26		7335											
St. Austell						6 24		9622									8 45		
Burngullow								7 00											
Grampound Road								7 27											
Probus and Ladock Platform								7 36											
Truro 116 ......arr.						6 47		7 49									9 8		
116 FALMOUTH ......arr.								9 5									10 4		
Truro ......dep.					6 0	6 52		7 5	7 55						8 15		9 13		
Chacewater 50					6 13			7 18	8 8						8 28				
Scorrier								7 24	8 15										
Redruth						7 14		7 31	8 22								9 33		
Carn Brea								7 36	8 28										
Camborne						7 24		7 42	8 34								9 43		
Gwinear Road 39						7 31		7 48	8 40								9 48		
39 HELSTON ......arr.								8 27	9 45										
Hayle								7 56	8 48								9 55		
St. Erth 39						7 43		8 2	8 55										
39 ST. IVES ......arr.						8 3			9 20										
Marazion								8 12	9 5								10 5		
Penzance ** ......arr.						7 55		8 17	9 10								10 10		

THE FALMOUTH HOTEL

This First-class Hotel stands in its own grounds of four acres, and has a magnificent view of the Bay and Pendennis Castle. Certificated Sanitary Arrangements.

PATRONISED BY H.M. THE KING WHEN PRINCE OF WALES.

ELECTRIC LIGHT.   AN OTIS ELEVATOR SERVES EACH FLOOR.

Tariff and full particulars on application to the Manager, C. DUPLESSY.

Main Line.]   25   [Great Western.

LONDON, READING, TAUNTON, EXETER, PLYMOUTH, and PENZANCE.—Great Western.

Down.	Week Days—Continued.	Sundays.

	aft	aft	aft	aft	aft	aft	aft	aft	aft	aft	aft	aft	Sat.	mrn	mrn	mrn	aft
12 PADDINGTON ..... dep.								4 15			6 30		10 0	1230			
12 Reading .... "								3931			6 12		1048	1 22			
12 Oxford .... "								2F12			6 2		1040			3 48	
12 Bath .... "	3 42							6 18			8 35		1240	3 27		4 17	
12 Bristol (Temp. Mds.) "	3 55							6 45			9 59 15		1 8	4 0		6 49	
Taunton .... dep.	5 10				5 35		7 42		8 20	10 2	1050		2 8	5 5		6 31	
Norton Fitzwarren					5 40				8 25		1055						
Wellington					5 52				8 36		11 5					8 45	
Burlescombe					6 2				8 46								
Tiverton Junction 50, 118..			5 45		6 13				8 56		1120					9 4	
Cullompton			5 51		6 20				9 2							9 16	
Hele and Bradninch			6 0		6 30				9 11								
Silverton			6 4		6 34				9 15								
Stoke Canon 51			6 14		6 44				9 24								
Exeter (St. David's) * { arr.	5 48		6 20		6 50		8 19		9 30	1040			2 46	5 45		9 33	
40 51,141,142,144 { dep.	5 55	6 10			7 5		8 26		9 35	1045			2 55	5 54 2 15	9 45	
Exeter (St. Thomas) 40		6 15			7 10				9 40								
Exminster		6 23			7 18				9 48								
Starcross †		6 31			7 26				9 56						9 2910 2	
Dawlish Warren		6 36			7 31												
Dawlish .... [Teignton	6 15	6 41			7 36		8 45		10 4				2 46		9 3810 14	
Teignmouth, for Bishop's	6 25	6 50			7 44		8 54		10 12	1113				6 229 46 1023	
Newton Abbot § 51 .... arr.	6 34	6 59			7 53		9 3		10 21	1122			5 23	6 31 9 55 1031	
51 Moretonhampsteadarr.	7 26																
51 Torquay .... "	7 6				8 18		9 36		11 3	1149				7 17 10 14 11 6	
51 Paignton .... "	7 13				8 27		9 46		11 12	1156				7 25 1029 1117	
51 Kingswear .... "					8 47		10 7		11 32					9 21	1138	
Newton Abbot .... dep.	6 40	7 7			8 10		9 10			1129			3 32	6 41	1042	
Totnes 57		7 26			8 28		9 28			1147				7 2	11 0	
Brent 54		7 46			8 46										1118	
54 Kingsbridge ...... arr.		8 45															
Wrangaton		7 52			8 52										1124	
Bittaford Platform		7 56														1128	
Ivybridge		8 1			9 3											1133	
Cornwood		8 6			9 8											1138	
Plympton		8 14			9 16											1146	
Plymouth (Mutley)		8 20			9 21									7 49	1152	
52, 142 (North Road) ..	7 28	8 23			9 24	m 10 5			1225			4 25	7 43		1154	m
(Millbay) ... arr.	7 38	m 8 31		m 9 33	m 1013				1235			4 55	7 53		12 5	m
Plymouth (Millbay) ..... dep.		8 15		8 45		10 5		10 50					7285 18			1210	
" (North Road)												4 35					
Devonport ‡		8 20		8 50		1010		10 58					7328 27			1215	
Keyham		8 26		8 56		1016		11 6					7368 32			1221	
St. Budeaux Platform		8 30		8 59		1019		11 10					7398 35			1224	
Saltash for Callington		8 36		9 2		1022		11 13					7448 40			1229	
Defiance Platform		8 38						11X17					8 43			1233	
St. Germans								11X27					7558 51				
Menheniot								11X38				5 9	8 49 2				
Liskeard 39								11X45					812 9 11				
39 Looe .... arr.																	
Doublebois													820 9 20				
Bodmin Road 47														9 31			
Lostwithiel 50														9 38			
Par 50												5 40		9 50			
50 Fowey .... arr.																	
50 Newquay .... "																	
St. Austell												5 55		10 3			
Burngullow																	
Grampound Road														1017			
Probus and Ladock Platform																	
Truro 116 .... arr.												6 18		1029			
116 Falmouth .... arr.														1117			
Truro .... dep.												6 26		1036			
Chacewater 50														1048			
Scorrier																	
Redruth												6 47		11 0			
Carn Brea																	
Camborne												6 58		1111			
Gwinear Road 39																	
39 Helston .... arr.																	
Hayle												7 14		1126			
St. Erth 39																	
39 St. Ives .... arr.																	
Marazion																	
Penzance ** .... arr.												7 26		1138			

LONDON, READING, TAUNTON, EXETER, PLYMOUTH, and PENZANCE.—Great Western.

Down.	Sundays—continued.														
	aft	aft	aft	aft	mrn	aft	aft	aft	aft	aft	aft	aft	aft	aft	aft
15 PADDINGTON. dep.					9 10					2 40				4 30	10 0
15 Reading ″					10 9				1248						1048
15 Oxford ″					9 55				1 15						9 40
15 Bath ″					1159				3 6					4 51	1235
15 Bristol (T. Mds.) ″					1245				4 15					7 0	1 8
	aft	aft	aft	aft	aft	aft	aft	aft	aft	aft	aft	aft	aft	aft	mrn
Taunton dep.					2 6				5 17	5 37					2 8
Norton Fitzwarren															
Wellington															
Burlescombe															
Tiverton Junction									Tea Car						Sleeping Car (1st Class).
Cullompton															
Hele and Bradninch															
Silverton															
Stoke Canon															
Exeter (St. Dav.)* 141, 142 arr.					2 45				5 55	6 16				8 35	2 46
Exeter (St. Dav.)* 141, 142 dep.				2 25	2 55	4 35			6 25			7 30		8 41	2 55
Exeter (St. Thomas)				2 30	3 1	4 39						7 35			
Exminster															
Starcross †				2 42	3 13	4 51						7 48			
Dawlish Warren				2 47	3 18	4 56	5 35					7 53			
Dawlish [Teignton	1235			2 52	3 24	5 0	5 39					7 58			
Teignmouth, for Bishop's	1242			3 0	3 33	5 8	5 46					8 7			n
Newton Abbot § 51 arr.	1251			3 9	3 42	5 17	5 55		6 51			8 16		9 9	3 23
Moretonhstead ar.															8 37
51 Torquay ″	1 11			3 31	4 23		6 16		7 27			8 47		9 43	4t10
51 Paignton ″	1 18			3 40	4 32		6 25		7 40			8 54		9 51	7 22
51 Kingswear ″					4 53				8 0						7 44
Newton Abbot dep.					3 52				7 0			8 25		9 17	3 32
Totnes					4 10							8 42			
Brent		1250			4 28							8 59			
Kingsbridge arr.															
Wrangaton		1256										9 5			
Bittaford Platform		1 0										9 9			
Ivybridge		1 5			4 40				Dining Car, Exeter to Plymouth.			9 14			
Cornwood		1 10										9 20			
Plympton		1 18			4 54							9 28			
Plymouth 52, 142 (Mutley)		1 24	m		5 0							9 34			
Plymouth (North Rd.)		1 27			5 3							9 37		10 7	4 25
Plymouth (Millbay) arr.		1 35			5 10			m	7 55		m	9 45		1015	4 55
Plymouth (Millbay) dep.			2 27					6 15			8 20		9 55		
″ (North Rd.)															4 35
Devonport ‡			2 32					6 20			8 25		10 3		
Keyham			2 38					6 26			8 31		1011		
St. Budeaux Platform			2 41		Luncheon Car to Exeter.			6 29			8 34		1015	Dining Car from Bristol.	
Saltash, for Callington			2 44					6 33			8 39		1020		
Defiance Platform			2 47					6 36	Exeter, Torquay, and Plymouth Express.						
St. Germans								6 45							
Menheniot															
Liskeard															5 9
Looe arr.															5 57
Doublebois															
Bodmin Road															5b24
Lostwithiel															
Par															5 40
Fowey arr.															6 52
Newquay ″															7 23
St. Austell															5 55
Burngullow															
Grampound Road															
Probus and Ladock Plat.															
Truro 116 arr.															6 18
116 Falmouth arr.															7 23
Truro dep.															6 26
Chacewater															
Scorrier															
Redruth															6 47
Carn Brea															
Camborne															6 58
Gwinear Road															7 7
Helston arr.															7 35
Hayle															7 15
St. Erth															7 23
St. Ives arr.															7 44
Marazion															b
Penzance ** arr.															7 40

NOTES.

- A Via Lostwithiel.
- n Stops at 3 12 mrn. on Mondays to take up.
- b Stops to set down only.
- B Via Chasewater, one class only.
- b Stops to set down from London on informing the Guard at Paddington.
- c Except Mondays.
- d Motor Car, one class only.
- F Via Reading.
- H Stops on Mondays to set down.
- h Passengers may secure Sleeping Car accommodation between Swindon and Penzance by notifying any Station Master en route before 3 aft. on the day required.
- i Via Devizes.
- J Leaves Oxford at 9 40 aft. and Bath at 12 35 ngt. on Sundays.
- m Motor Car, one class only.
- N Via North Road.
- s Saturdays only.
- t Torre Station.
- V By Slip Carriage.
- X Thursdays and Saturdays.

* Nearly 1 mile to Queen Street Station (L. & S. W.).
† Ferry to Exmouth (1¾ miles).
‡ Nearly ¾ mile to L. & S. W. Station.
§ Station for King's Teignton (1½ miles).

** For St. Just, Cape Cornwall, Land's End, and Scilly Isles.

Service of Road Motor Cars runs between Penzance Station and St. Just and Land's End.

*** For other Trains

BETWEEN	PAGE
London and Exeter	140
Taunton and Norton Fitzwarren	54
Stoke Canon and Exeter	51
Exeter and Plymouth	142
Plympton, Plymouth, and Defiance Platform	55
Plymouth and St. Budeaux	142, 143
Truro and Chacewater	50

POLDHU HOTEL,

Mullion, Cornwall.

First Class. Largest in District. Electric Light. Close to Sea. Good Beach. Bathing and Boating.

CLOSE TO AND NEAREST TO SPLENDID GOLF LINKS (18 holes).

Motor Garage. Station—Helston. Apply MANAGER.

PENZANCE, PLYMOUTH, EXETER, TAUNTON, READING, and LONDON.—Great Western.

Week Days.

Miles	Up.	mrn	mrn	mrn	mrn	mrn	mrn	mrn	mrn	mrn		mrn	mrn	mrn	mrn	mrn	mrn	mrn		mrn	mrn
				Through Carriages, Plymouth to Liverpool, also Kingswear to Manchester, see pages 51, 18, and 452.					Breakfast and Luncheon Car, Plymouth to Paddington. Plymouth and Torquay Exp.		Through Carriages, Plymouth to Liverpool, see pages 18, and 452. Through Carriages, Plymouth to Glasgow and Aberdeen via Severn Tunnel, Crewe, and Carlisle, see pages 18, 452, 414a, and 828; also Torquay to Manchester, see pages 18, 452, and 478, and to Leeds and Bradford, see pages 631 and 610.—	Breakfast, Luncheon, and Tea Car, Plymouth to Liverpool (Lime Street).	Mondays and Thursdays; also on 1st Tuesday in the month.						Through Carriages, Plymouth to Birkenhead, Liverpool, Birmingham (Snow Hill), and Wolverhampton, and Kingswear to Birmingham (Snow Hill) and Manchester, see pages 51, 18, 108, 106, and 85.	Luncheon, Tea, and Dining Car, Plymouth to Liverpool (Lime Street).	From Newquay
	Penzance dep.																				
2	Marazion																				
—	39 St. Ives dep.																				
5¾	St. Erth 39																				
7¼	Hayle																				
—	39 Helston dep.																				
10¾	Gwinear Road 39																				
13¼	Camborne																				
14¾	Carn Brea																				
16¾	Redruth																				mrn
19	Scorrier																				8 46
20¾	Chacewater 50																				8 57
26	Truro 116 arr.																				Stop
—	116 Falmouth dep.																7 0				
—	Truro dep.																7 50				
31	Probus and Ladock Platform																				
33½	Grampound Road																8 6				
38	Burngullow																8 16				
40¼	St. Austell																8 22				
—	50 Newquay dep.																				
—	50 Fowey "																8 10				
45	Par 50												8 4				8 31				
49½	Lostwithiel 50												8 14				8 42				
52¾	Bodmin Road 47												Stop				8 52				
58½	Doublebois																9 9				
—	39 Looe dep.							6 45									8 25				
61¾	Liskeard 39							7 30									9 17				
65	Menheniot							7 39													
70½	St. Germans							7 43		mrn							9 33				
74¼	Defiance Platform					mrn		7 56		8 12				mrn				mrn			
75¼	Saltash (for Callington)					6 50		8 2		8 16				8 35			9 42	10 0			
76½	St. Budeaux Platform		mrn			6 54		8 5		8 20				8 38				10 3			
77¼	Keyham		6 45			6 57		8 8		8 23				8 42				10 8			
78¼	Devonport‡		6 51			7 3		8 14		8 30				8 51			9 51	1015			
79½	Plymouth (North Road)		6 54											8 58				1019			
80½	52, 142 (Millbay) arr.					7 8		8 18		8 36							9 56				
—	Plymouth (Millbay) dep.			7 10		Stop	7 30		8 30			8 40			9 23					1025	
—	" (North Road)		6 56				7 35							9 0	9 28			1020			
80	" (Mutley)		6 58	7 17			7 38		8 36			8 47		9 2	9 31			1022		1032	
83½	Plympton		Stop				7 46							Stop	9 39						
88	Cornwood						8 0								9 53						
90¼	Ivybridge						8 6								9 59						
92½	Bittaford Platform						8 11								10 4						
93¾	Wrangaton						8 15								10 8						
—	54 Kingsbridge dep.						7 25								9 30						
95¾	Brent 54						8 23								1016						
102¾	Totnes 57			7 52			8 37					9 24			1030						
111½	Newton Abbot§ 51 arr.		mrn	8 7			8 52		9 24			9 39			1045					1119	
—	51 Kingswear dep.		6 30	6 30		mrn			8 25			8 25				9 30				1020	
—	51 Paignton "		6 53	6 53		8 10			8 51			9 16				9 58				1045	
—	51 Torquay "		7 0	7 0		8 18			9 1			9 23				10 6				1055	
—	51 Moretonhampstead "					7 55						9 0				mrn					mrn
—	Newton Abbot dep.		7 40	8 12		8 45			9 31			9 48				1050				1128	1145
116½	Teignmouth, for Bishop's Teignton		7 51	8 23		8 56			9 43			10 0				11 4				1142	1156
119½	Dawlish		8 0	8 33		9 4			9 52			1010				1112				1153	12 4
120¾	Dawlish Warren		8 4			9 8										1116					12 8
123	Starcross †		8 9			9 14										1123					1214
126¾	Exminster		8 17			9 22										1131					1222
130¾	Exeter (St. Thomas) 40		8 27			9 32										1140					1232
131½	Exeter (St. David's)* arr.		8 30	8 50		9 35			10 9			1027		mrn		1143				1210	1235
	40, 51, 141, 142, 144 dep.	8 5		8 58	9 10				10 15			1033		11 0						1220	
135	Stoke Canon	8 12			9 17									11 7							
138¾	Silverton	8 19			9 24									1114							
140	Hele and Bradninch	8 23			9 28									1118							
144½	Cullompton	8 33			9 38									1128							
146¾	Tiverton Junction 50, 118	8 43			9 48									1138							
150¾	Burlescombe	8 53			9 58								mrn	1148							
155¼	Wellington	9 4			10 9								1110	1159							
160½	Norton Fitzwarren 54	9 14			1019									12 9							
162¾	Taunton 7, 17, 54 arr.	9 18		9 35	1023				10 53			1112	1120	1213						1 0	
207	17 Bristol (Temp. Mds.) arr.			1050								1225		1 34						2 11	
218¾	17 Bath "			1125								1 d 8		2 2						2 47	
281¼	17 Oxford "								12 42											5 21	
269¼	17 Reading "								12‖53					3‖26						5 16	
305¼	17 PADDINGTON "								1 30					4 5							

For Notes, see page 31; for Continuation of Trains, see pages 28 to 31.

THE FOWEY HOTEL.

This Hotel is situate overlooking the picturesque Harbour of Fowey, with charming views of the English Channel.
Smoking Lounge.　Large Coffee and Dining Room.　Reading Room.　Ladies' Drawing Room, &c.
THE ENTIRE BUILDING IS LIGHTED BY ELECTRICITY.　BILLIARDS.　LAWN TENNIS AND CROQUET.
N.B.—Boating, Bathing, and Excellent Sea and River Fishing.　**Apply to the MANAGERESS.**
Golf Links within a mile from the Hotel.
THE HOTEL PROPERTY INCLUDES PRIVATE LANDING SLIPS AND BATHING COVES.

PENZANCE, PLYMOUTH, EXETER, TAUNTON, READING, and LONDON.—Great Western.

Up.　　　　Week Days—*Continued.*

	mrn	mrn	mrn	mrn	mrn	mrn	mrn	mrn	mrn	aft	aft	aft	aft		aft	aft	aft	mrn	mrn
Penzance..........dep.					8 0			9 10	10 0									1030	11 0
Marazion..........					8 8			9 16										1036	11 6
39 St. Ives..........dep.				7 55			8 41	9 40										1025	....
St. Erth 39				8 18			9 25	1016										1047	1116
Hayle..........				8 23			9 29											1052	....
39 Helston..........dep.				7 55				9 45										....	....
Gwinear Road 39				8 34			9 40	1030										11 3	....
Camborne..........				8 42	9 25		9 48											1111	1134
Carn Brea..........				8 48	9 30		9 53											1120	1143
Redruth..........				8 56	9 36		9 59											1128	....
Scorrier..........				9 1	9 41		10 4											1128	1158
Chacewater 50				9 7	9 47	9 58	10 9											1138	....
Truro 116..........arr.				9 16	9 56	10 8	1018	1056										1040	1120
116 Falmouth..........dep.				8 30			Stop	Stop	1010									....	....
Truro..........dep.				9 22				11 2										1145	12 6
Probus and Ladock Platform				9 31														....	....
Grampound Road..........				9 41														....	....
Burngullow..........				9 52														1211	1233
St. Austell..........				9 59														....	....
50 Newquay..........dep.				9 0														1110	....
60 Fowey.........."				9 55														1150	....
Par 50				10 8														1222	1247
Lostwithiel 50				1020														....	1259
Bodmin Road 47				1030														1238	....
Doublebois..........				1045														....	....
39 Looe..........dep.				1010														1215	....
Liskeard 39	9 35			1054														1250	1 24
Menheniot..........	9 46			11 2	mrn									1245				....	....
St. Germans..........	9 58			1112										1255				....	....
Defiance Platform		mrn			1138													....	....
Saltash (for Callington)	1010	1055		1121	1140					1230								1 4	....
St. Budeaux Platform		1058			1144						1233							1 8	....
Keyham..........	1017	11 1		1126	1146						1236							1 16	....
Devonport!..........	1020	11 6		1131	1152						1236	1242						1 22	....
Plymouth (North Road) ..				1137	1157			aft	1223									1 30	1 50
52, 142 (Millbay).....arr.	1031	1110									1242	1247						1 33	1 50
Plymouth (Millbay)...dep.			1115	1120				1210		1240								1 25	....
" (North Road)....	Stop	Stop	1121	1125				1215	1230	1245				1 10				1 40	....
" (Mutley)....			1128					1217						1 10				....	....
Plympton..........			1136					1228		1252								....	....
Cornwood..........			1161							1 6								....	....
Ivybridge..........			1157							1 12								....	....
Bittaford Platform			12 3							1 17								....	....
Wrangaton..........			12 8							1538								....	....
54 Kingsbridge..........dep.			11 0															....	....
Brent 54			1155	1215						1 45								....	....
Totnes 57			1228							2 0								....	....
Newton Abbot §51 .....arr.			1218	1243						2 15								....	....
51 Kingswear..........dep.			1130							1250					1 10			....	....
51 Paignton.........."			1157	1212						1241					1 35			....	....
51 Torquay.........."			1210	1218						1249					1 35			....	....
51 Moretonhampstead. "		aft	1133												1 35			....	....
Newton Abbot..........dep.		mrn	1230	1250						1 25					2 8			....	....
Teignmouth, for Bishop's..		1250		1 5						1 37					2 15			....	....
Dawlish..........[Teignton		1258								1 46								....	....
Dawlish Warren		1 2																....	....
Starcross!..........										1 35	1452							....	....
Exminster!..........										1 41								....	....
Exeter (St. Thomas) 40										1 49	2 6							....	....
Exeter (St. David's) { arr.	aft									1 38	1 58	2 10						....	....
40,51,141,142,144 { dep.	1 0		1 26							1 45	2 2							....	....
StokeCanon..........	1 7																	....	....
Silverton..........	1 14																	....	....
Hele and Bradninch	1 18																	....	....
Cullompton..........	1 27																	....	....
Tiverton Junction 50, 118..	1 36																	....	....
Burlescombe..........	1 46																	....	....
Wellington..........	1 57																	....	....
Norton Fitzwarren 54																		....	....
Taunton 7, 17, 54 .....arr.	2 7																	....	....
17 Bristol (Temp. Mds.) arr.										3 4								4 5	....
17 Bath.......... "										4 0								5 23	....
17 Oxford.......... "										4 33								7 0	....
17 Reading.......... "																		7 23	....
17 Paddington.......... "			3 55							4 45						6 25		6 50	....

GREAT WESTERN RAILWAY.
TREGENNA CASTLE HOTEL,
ST. IVES, CORNWALL.

THIS well-known castellated Mansion, the ancient seat of the Stephen family, is situated amidst forest trees overlooking St. Ives Bay, 350 feet above sea level, in its own grounds of nearly 100 acres. Dairy Produce from pedigree Guernsey herd on the estate. The prospect from this elevation is charming, and the air bracing.

Luxurious Lounge. Billiard Room. Library and Reading Room. Electric Light throughout. Lawn Tennis. Croquet. Bowls.

The famous West Cornwall Golf Course is within easy reach of the Hotel.

Telephone: 38 St. Ives. Visitors can communicate from the Hotel by Telephone with all the Trunk Lines.
Telegraphic Address: "Tregotel," St. Ives, Cornwall.
Tariff and full particulars can be obtained on application to the Hotel Manager.

PENZANCE, PLYMOUTH, EXETER, TAUNTON, READING, and LONDON.—Great Western

Up.

Week Days—*Continued.*

	aft	mrn	aft	aft	aft		non	aft	aft	aft	aft	aft	aft	aft	aft	aft	aft	aft	aft
Penzance....dep.							12 0	1245								2 0			
Marazion........							12 6	1250											
3⁹ St. Ives....dep.							1150	1245								1 50			
St. Erth 39........							1218	1 3								2 16			
Hayle............							1223	1 10								2 21			
39 Helston....dep.							1155									1 45			
Gwinear Road 39							1236	1 20								2 32			
Camborne........							1243	1 27								2 39			
Carn Brea........							1249	1 33								2 44			
Redruth..........							1256	1 39								2 50			
Scorrier..........				1219			1 3	1 45								2 56	aft		
Chacewater 50...				1219			1 9	1 52								3 2	3 10		
Truro 116....arr.				1230			1 19	2 2								3 11	3 22		
116 Falmouth....dep.		1120	Stop				1235	Stop								1 35	Stop		
Truro........dep.		1215					1 26									3 17			
Probus and Ladock Platform		1224														3 27			
Grampound Road..		1233					1 42									3 35			
Burngullow......		1243					1 52									3 45			
St. Austell......		1249					1 59									3 51			
50 Newquay....dep.							1240									2 50			
50 Fowey........ "							10									340			
Par 50..........		1258					2 9									4 1			
Lostwithiel 50 ..							2 12									4 12			
Bodmin Road 47..							2 24									4 22			
Doublebois........							2 35									4 38			
39 Looe....dep.							2 50									4 0			
Liskeard 39......							2 58									4 48			
Menheniot																4 55			
St. Germans........	aft						3 14		aft	aft						5 6			
Defiance Platform....	1 50								3 33	3 52									
Saltash, for Callington	1 53			3 5			3 25		3 37	3 55			4 8			5 17		6 20	
St. Budeaux Platform	1 56			3 9					3 41				4 11			5 21		6 24	
Keyham............	1 59			3 12					3 45	4			4 14			5 26		6 28	
Devonport }	2 5			3 17			37		3 51	4			4 21			5 33		6 34	
Plymouth (North Road).. "							3 40			4 8									
52, 142 (Millbay)....arr.	2 10			3 32					3 56				4 26			5 39		6 39	
Plymouth (Millbay)....dep.	Stop			2 20			3430						4 20	5 5		5 58		7 5	
" (North Road) "				2 23			3 55	4 10					4 26	5 10		6 4		7 11	
" (Mutley)........				2 28									4 29	5 12		6 7		7 14	
Plympton............				2 36									4 37	5 20		6 15		7 22	
Cornwood............				2 50									4 51	5 34		6 30		7 37	
Ivybridge............				2 56									4 57	5 39		6 36		7 43	
Bittaford Platform				3 1									5 2	5 44		6 42		7 49	
Wrangaton........				3 5									5 7	5 49		6 47		7 54	
54 Kingsbridge....dep.				2 25									4 10	4 10					6 55
Brent 54............				3 14									5 15	5 56		6 55		8 2	
Totnes 57............				3 28									5 31	6 12		7 10		8 17	
Newton Abbot § 51....arr.			aft	3 43			4 45	4 58					5 46	6 27		7 26		8 32	
51 Kingswear........dep.				2 25			3 50	3 50			aft	4 50				6 25			
51 Paignton........				2 47	3 25			164	16			4 05	14		6 6	6 54		8 5	
51 Torquay........				2 53	3 33			4 24	4 24			4 48	22		6 8	7 3		8 12	
51 Moretonhampstead. "								4 20				4 20				6 45			
Newton Abbot....dep.				3 20	4 5			4 51	5 8			5 20	0		6 38	7 35		8 42	
Teignmouth, for Bishop's				3 32	4 17							5 34	6 12		6 51	7 49		8 53	
Dawlish..........[Teignton				3 42	4 25							5 42	6 21		7 0	7 58		9 1	
Dawlish Warren......				3 44	4 29							5 46	6 25		7 4	8 2		9 4	
Starcross †........				3 50	4 38							5 52	6 31		7 10	8 8		9 9	
Exminster............				3 59	4 44							6 1	6 40			8 16		9 17	
Exeter (St. Thomas) 40 ..			aft	4 9	4 54							6 11	6 51		7 25	8 26		9 27	
Exeter (St. David's) * { arr.	aft		4 12	4 57								6 15	6 54		7 28	8 29	aft	9 30	
40, 51, 141, 142, 144 { dep.	3 43		4 20				4 17	5 34	aft			7 10					9 20		
Stoke Canon........	3 50		4 27				25	4 25	5 50			7 19					b		
Silverton............	3 57		4 34						5 57			7 27					b		
Hele and Bradninch....	4 1		4 39					6 4				7 32					9 38		
Cullompton........	4 10		4 48					6 19				7 45					9 48		
Tiverton Junction 50, 118..	4 20		4 54					6735				7 59					9 56		
Burlescombe........	4 30							6 45				8 9							
Wellington............								6 58				8 23							
Norton Fitzwarren 54 ..	4 52							7 8											
Taunton 7, 17, 54....arr.	4 56						6 56	207	12			8 33					1021		
17 Bristol (Temp. Mds.) arr.							7 37	22				1040							
17 Bath............ "							7 49					1112							
17 Oxford.......... "							9 47												
17 Reading........ "							9 35					1 47							
17 Paddington...... "							1025					2 45							

For Notes, see page 31; for Continuation of Trains, see pages 30 and 31.

ROUGEMONT HOTEL.

PATRONIZED BY ROYALTY.

THE LARGEST and ONLY MODERN HOTEL IN EXETER. Near Railway Stations. Beautiful Lounge Hall.
Spacious Coffee Room. Omnibus meets all Trains. Night Porter. Garage, with Inspection Pit. Electric Lift.

Apply Manager.

Telegrams. "ROUGEMONT, EXETER." Telephone: **433.**

PENZANCE, PLYMOUTH, EXETER, TAUNTON, READING, and LONDON.—Great Western.

Up		Week Days—Continued.													Sundays.						
	aft	aft	aft	aft	aft	aft	aft	aft	aft	aft	aft	aft	aft	aft	mrn	mrn	mrn	mrn	mrn	mrn	mrn
Penzance................dep.			4 15					6 15	7 15					8 40							
Marazion........................			4 23					6 22	7 21					8 47							
39 ST. IVES...........dep.	m		4 5					5 45	7 5					8 35							
St. Erth 39	4 3		4 32					6 31	7 30					8 56							
Hayle	4 7		4 37					6 35	7 35					9 1							
39 HELSTON ....dep.			3 55					5 28	6 55					8 35							
Gwinear Road 39	4 17		4 48					6 46	7 46					9 12							
Camborne.....................	4 24		4 55					6 53	7 53					9 19							
Carn Brea....................	4 29							6 58													
Redruth.......................	4 34		5 5					7 3	8 3					9 29							
Scorrier......................	4 39			m		m		7 9			m			9 34							
Chacewater 50	4 45		5 14	5 44		7 4		7 18	8 12		8 30			9 40							
Truro 116 ....arr.	4 55		5 23	5 56		7 15		7 24	8 21		8 42			9 49							
116 FALMOUTH.........dep.			4 30					6 8					Stop	9 15							
Truro........................dep.			5 31					7 32						9 56							
Probus and Ladock Platform			5 41																		
Grampound Road............			5 50					7 47													
Burngullow...................								7 56													
St. Austell...................			6 5					8 2					1023								
50 NEWQUAY...........dep.			4 55					6 25					7935								
50 FOWEY.............. "			5 35					7050					9 10								
Par 50			6 16					8 11					1033								
Lostwithiel 50			6 27					8 21					1044								
Bodmin Road 47			6 37					8 30													
Doublebois...................								8 45						8 40							
39 LOOE..............dep.			5 45					7 15													
Liskeard 39..................			6 59					8 52					11 9		8 54						
Menheniot....................								9 0							9 9						
St. Germans..................	6 50	7 15	m		m			9 9		aft					9 23		m				
Defiance Platform	6 58		7 31		8 42					m							1040				
Saltash (for Callington).....	7 1	7 27	34		8 44		9 19			9 42		1030			9 36		1045				
St. Budeaux Platform........	7 4		7 38		8 48					9 46		1034			9 40		1046				
Keyham	7 8		7 41		8 51			9 24		9 49		1037			9 44		1050				
Devonport ‡..................	7 10	7 35	7 47		8 59			9 30		9 55		1043	1140		9 52		1056				
Plymouth (North Road)......	7 41																				
52, 142 (Millbay) .....arr.	7 20		7 52		9 2			9 36		10 0	m	1048	1145		9 56		11 1				m
Plymouth (Millbay) ....dep.			7 35				9 15				1045		1215	7 0		1010		11 4			1150
" (North Road) "			8 0				9 20				1049							11 7			1135
" (Mutley) "							9 23				1050			7 7		1019		11 9			1137
Plympton.....................							9 31				11 1							1121			1144
Cornwood.....................							9 45				1115										1158
Ivybridge.....................							9 51				1122			7 34							12 4
Bittaford Platform...........											1128										1210
Wrangaton....................							9 58				1133										1215
54 KINGSBRIDGE.......dep.																					
Brent 54.....................							10 5				1138				7 47						1220
Totnes 57....................			8 42				1019								8 4						
Newton Abbot § 51 .....arr.			8 57				1034							1 12	8 19		11 5				
51 KINGSWEAR.........dep.			8 0					1035				1635				9 45	9 45				
51 PAIGNTON .... "			8 23					1056				1245	7 40			1040	1040		12 5		
51 TORQUAY............ "			8 30					11 3				1253	7 50			1048	1048		1212		
51 MORETONHAMPSTEAD. "			8810																		
Newton Abbot ....dep.			9 8					1130				1 23	8 29		1115	1125		1233			
Teignmouth, for Bishop's			9 20					1140					8 41			1135		1244			
Dawlish............(Teignton)			9 30					1146					8 50			1141		1252			
Dawlish Warren.............																					
Starcross †...................													9 3				1 0				
Exminster....................																					
Exeter (St. Thomas) 40.																					
Exeter (St. David's) * { arr.			9 47									1 50	9 15			1142		1 12			
40,51,141,142,144 { dep			9 57									1 57	9 25			1150					
Stoke Canon.................																					
Silverton.....................																					
Hele and Bradninch.........																					
Cullompton...................														9 46							
Tiverton Junction 50, 118..														9 58							
Burlescombe..................																					
Wellington....................														1015							
Norton Fitzwarren 54																					
Taunton 7, 17, 54.....arr.			1036											2 36	1025						
17 BRISTOL (Temp. Mds.) arr.			1155											3 47	1210		1 30				
17 BATH................... "														4 23	1248		3 50				
17 OXFORD................ "														7915			3 32				
17 READING............... "														6 12	2 42		4 45				
17 PADDINGTON........ "														7 10	3 55		4 5				

PENZANCE, PLYMOUTH, EXETER, TAUNTON, READING, and LONDON.—Great Western.

Up. — **Sundays**—*Continued.*

	aft	aft	aft	f mrn	aft	aft	aft	aft	aft	aft	ngt.
Penzance ....dep.				11 10					4 40		
Marazion											
St. Ives ....dep.											
St. Erth				11 23					4 53		
Hayle											
Helston ....dep.											
Gwinear Road.....											
Camborne........				11 42					5 11		
Carn Brea........											
Redruth				11 52					5 21		
Scorrier											
Chacewater.....				11 59					5 29		
Truro 116. ....arr.				12 10					5 40		
116 Falmouth ....dep.				11 30					5 0		
Truro ....dep.				12 15					5 47		
Probus and Ladock Platform											
Grampound Road..				12 29					6 3		
Burngullow........											
St. Austell........				12 44					6 18		
Newquay ....dep.											
Fowey .... "											
Par.....				12 53					6 28		
Lostwithiel				1 4					6 40		
Bodmin Road.....				1 13					6 50		
Doublebois.....				1 23							
Looe ....dep.											
Liskeard				1 35					7 14		
Menheniot											
St. Germans			111	1 52		111			6 50	7 31	
Defiance Platform			1243		4 57				6 59	...	
Saltash (for Callington)			1245	2 2	5 0			7 2	1030	
St. Budeaux Platform			1248		5 3			7 5	1033	
Keyham			1252		5 7			7 9	1036	
Devonport ‡			1258	2 12	5 13			7 15	1041	
Plymouth (North Road)				2 15					5 0	1047	
52, 142 (Millbay) ..arr.	1 5				5 18			7 20		
Plymouth (Millbay) ..dep.	1 0					5 40			7 50	1215	
" (North Road)	1 7			2 30		5 45			8 15		
" (Mutley)						5 47					
Plympton						5 54					
Cornwood						6 8					
Ivybridge						6 14			11		
Bittaford Platform						6 20					
Wrangaton*						6 25					
Kingsbridge ....dep.											
Brent						6 31					
Totnes						6 45			8 57		
Newton Abbot § 51 ...arr.	1 57			3 20		7 0			9 12	1 12	
51 Kingswear...dep.	1 0		1 0	1 0		5 55			8 20		
51 Paignton ..... "	1 24		2 15	2 50	4 30	6 17	7 41		8 40	1010	
51 Torquay ..... "	1 34		2 25	3 0	4 37	6 25	7 50		8 50	1018	
51 Moretonhampstead "											
Newton Abbot ....dep.	2 8		2 50	3 30	5 1	7 10	8 15		9 59	1 23	
Teignmouth, for Bishop's	2 21		3 1		5 12	7 21	8 26		9 32		
Dawlish ......(Teignton)	2 26		3 9		5 20	7 29	8 34		9 46		
Dawlish Warren			3 15		5 23	7 33	8 38				
Starcross †			3 18			7 38	8 43				
Exminster											
Exeter (St. Thomas)			3 32			7 52	8 57				
Exeter (St. David's) * { arr.	2 53		3 35	3 57		7 55	9 0		10 3	1 50	
141, 142 { dep.	3 2			4 5					1010	1 57	
Stoke Canon											
Silverton											
Hele and Bradninch											
Cullompton											
Tiverton Junction											
Burlescombe											
Wellington											
Norton Fitzwarren											
Taunton 11, 21 .....arr.	3 41			4 43					1049	2 36	
21 Bristol (Temp. Mds.) arr.	5 17			6 45					1157	3 47	
21 Bath ..... "	5 48			8 58					1238	4 23	
21 Oxford .... "				9 47						7 15	
21 Reading .... "				9 45					2 25	6 12	
21 Paddington .... "				7 45					3 15	7 10	

NOTES.

a Arrives Wrangaton at 1 21 aft.

A Via Westbury.

B Via Reading, Slip Carriage Taunton to Reading.

b Stops to set down.

d Motor Car, one class only.

h Passengers may secure Sleeping Car accommodation between York and Aberdeen (Saturday nights excepted) by notifying any Station Master en route before 3 aft. on the day required.

J Via Lostwithiel.

m Motor Car, one class only.

n Stops at 8 35 aft. to take up for London on notice being given to the Station Master not later than 7 aft.

P Via Chacewater.

s Saturdays only.

T Arrives Tiverton Junction at 6 25 aft.

u Arrives Oxford at 11 5 mrn. on Sundays.

V Via Westbury and Swindon.

* Nearly 1 mile to Queen Street Station (L. & S. W.).

† Ferry to Exmouth (1¾ miles).

‡ Nearly ¾ mile to L. & S. W. Station.

§ Station for King's Teignton (1¾ miles).

‖ Slip Carriage.

** For other Trains

BETWEEN	PAGE
Chacewater and Truro..	50
St. Budeaux and Plymouth	142, 143
Defiance Platform, Plymouth and Plympton	55
Plymouth and Exeter...	142
Exeter and London	141
Exeter and Stoke Canon	51
Norton Fitzwarren and Taunton............	54

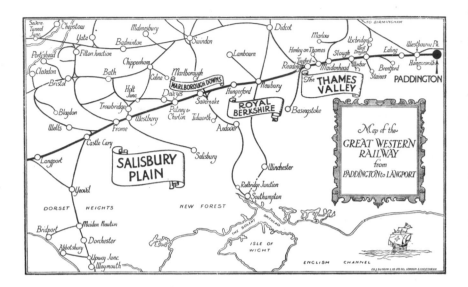

Map of the
GREAT WESTERN
RAILWAY
from
PADDINGTON to LANGPORT

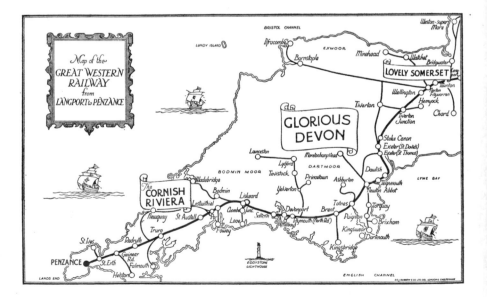

Map of the
GREAT WESTERN
RAILWAY
from
LANGPORT to PENZANCE